The Kayak Coaches' Manifesto

An Alternative Approach to High Performance Kayaking

Dari Y. Fisher
B.H.K., B.Ed.

Published by:

FriesenPress
Suite 300 – 852 Fort Street
Victoria, BC, Canada V8W 1H8

www.friesenpress.com

Distributed to the trade by The Ingram Book Company

Table of Contents

Forward

Upon reading this book, I felt an immediate and certain "déjà vu", because the basic theory is extremely similar to that which my former coach taught me when I was a beginner athlete. In the fall of 1969 my coach was Imre Kemecsey. He is one of those rare individuals who has had an outstanding career as an athlete. Later, he became a great coach, and he raised a series of champions.

Imre's innovative thinking has always been far ahead of his time, and he is constantly looking for new solutions. These help to better understand the secrets of kayaking, which in turn, assist in producing more proficient athletes.

Years later, during my time spent coaching in Norway, I instinctively used many of Imre's teachings as training methods, particularly in the area of technical concepts. _It seems clear that I have been "vaccinated" with Kemecsey for my lifetime!_

A few years ago, I was fortunate enough to have the opportunity to lecture on his first book, **The Inner Structure of the Kayak Technique**, and I thoroughly enjoyed the opportunity of working with Imre yet again! He brought new ideas and definitions into the kayak technique, such as **power circles** and **tensegrity**. These have opened new lines of communication for our beloved sport, and these ideas have been embraced by a growing number of coaches.

This book, entitled **The Kayak Coaches' Manifesto,** authored by Dari Y. Fisher, is a precise summary of all that today's coaches need to know in order to provide the best information to their developing athletes. It offers many answers and solutions for coaches in their daily work.

We have been awaiting this manual for a long time!

Thank you, Imre and Dari!

Zoltán Bako
5X World Champion, Olympic Medalist
M.Sc. in canoe-kayak
Former Coach of Knut Holmann and Eirik Verås Larsen *(Olympic Gold Medalists)*
Leader Lecturer of the *International Canoe Federation Intensive Course for Canoe-Kayak* Coaches - Level 3

Preface – "Paddles Up, Take it Away!"

As an athlete, coach, personal trainer, and teacher, I have been involved at various levels in the extraordinary sports of flatwater and surfski kayaking for approximately 20 years. Kayaking is an endeavour for which I have developed a great passion, and I am extremely eager to share my thoughts and ideas with any and all readers of this book. It should be noted that the subsequent concepts that I intend to divulge have been developed primarily by trial and error in consultation with Dr. Imre Kemecsey*. Perhaps it will be possible at a future date to scientifically prove many of these theories. Nevertheless, at this point in time, I willingly challenge any potential detractors to disprove these theories.

Over the years, I have read many articles and sport science publications that have, in a biomechanical fashion, attempted to fully analyze and uncover the technical intricacies involved in enhancing performance for a specific or particular sport. Although science obviously has played, and continues to play, a major role in going faster, flying higher and being stronger (the Olympic Motto - Citius, Altius, Fortius), I believe that an over-reliance on biomechanical principles has countless limitations and may, on occasion, even prove to be counter-productive. I am strongly of the opinion that I am not committing treason or treachery of any sort based on that which I am about to declare. Nevertheless, numerous theoretical factors may play an equally important role in discreet harmony with empirical factors. Obviously critical analyses of levers, forces, angles, and percentages can be useful in a laboratory setting, and may, at times, prove helpful to the athlete. Nevertheless, it is my staunch opinion that we are fooling ourselves, more often than not, into believing that this, alone, is the "holy grail" to success in sport. In terms of published literature, it has, for the most part, been comprised of writer upon writer saying the same thing in a slightly different version (i.e. nothing new and progressive.) We do not need to hear, yet again, about **rotation**, **sitting up**, or **using the large muscles in the back** for the umpteenth time. There is so much more to kayaking than elementary, superficial, and basic biomechanical tips. Utilizing only this method of coaching does not do this great sport justice, and has the potential, ultimately, of inhibiting an athlete's ability to "step forward" to the next level.

It is a normal behavioural trait to refute that which cannot be easily quantified in an objective manner. It is also natural to have an apprehension or fear with respect to what we do not fully understand. Furthermore, I should mention that I have conversed with many coaches who agree with these pedagogical methods which I espouse. However, it is unfortunate that others, without a factual understanding, refer to these philosophies and modalities as **old school**. In my many years involved in this superb sport, I have never met anyone who takes the progressive, dynamic, and forward-thinking approach as does Dr. Imre Kemecsey. He was, and is, a bona fide trailblazer... years ahead of his time!

The following information may seem to be extremely unorthodox and/or foreign to many who attempt to master these technical and structural aspects of kayaking. For some, various mental pictures will be quite easy to grasp, while for others this can be quite a challenge. Ultimately, however, if athletes and coaches alike embrace these concepts and persevere, I believe that over time substantial gains are inevitable, despite the potential for the occasional temporary setback.

In précis, the ultimate question is, "In what manner can athletes be best assisted to improve upon their times and/or speed?" My response is that we must demand from ourselves the adoption and adaptation of an athlete-centered and open-minded philosophy, whereby we empower our athletes with the ability to choose as to whether or not these concepts must be given credence. Based upon my many experiences, the results will dramatically speak for themselves. As the great Albert Einstein once said, "If at first, the idea is not absurd, then there is no hope for it!"

*Dr. Imre Kemecsey – Master Coach, Sport Psychologist, and Olympic Silver Medalist (Rome, 1960)

Acknowledgements

I am deeply grateful to all who have assisted me with various aspects geared toward the completion of this book. Without them, this project might never have reached fruition. To my family, thank you for showing interest and keeping me on task; to all my past coaches, teammates, and fellow competitors, thank you for pushing me to the limits of my capacities and capabilities in many dimensions. Much appreciation must also be given to my home club, The Burnaby Canoe and Kayak Club. To my work/teacher colleague, May Szeto, thank you for listening to me over the last few years with an open mind and heart. I extend much gratitude to Dave Marchant for his knowledge and insight; to Jodi Boates for her expertise and experience in the gym; and to Steve Juranovics, my current training partner and trusted friend. Last, but certainly not least, an enormous amount of appreciation and gratitude is extended to my devoted coach, Imre Kemecsey, for his guidance, mentorship, care, ideas, and faith, with which he has entrusted me. Imre, for all you have imparted to me, this book is my tribute to your methods!

Chapter 1
Development of a Kayaking Philosophy

Over the past ten years or so, I have contemplated writing a manual with respect to coaching high performance kayaking to both emerging and elite athletes. Up until very recently I lacked the discipline and drive to actually turn this desire into action. In hindsight, I must say I am pleased I waited! During these past ten years, in particular, I have had the opportunity to further reflect and conceptualize on the manner in which to go about completing this arduous task. Initially, I thought about writing a book on the subject of kayaking in general; however, a quote I once heard, "A book about everything is a book about nothing", kept resonating and resounding. Although I do not agree in totality with this statement, I do not feel free to abandon it either. I know that, in essence, I would far rather write in a precise manner about a small number of focused topics, as opposed to writing vaguely about a multitude of topics. I point out that the tagline for this book, "*An Alternative Holistic, Technical, Structural, and Pedagogical Approach to High Performance Kayaking*" was not decided upon hastily or arbitrarily. The *holistic* methodology refers to the simple fact that no single component of paddling works in isolation. The whole is greater than the sum of its parts. The more one does correctly, the more will ultimately be correct, and vice versa. The words *technical* and *structural* are utilized in unison, due to the fact that kayaking requires more than just good technique; rather, the excellent paddler must also develop a *sound* posture, just as would be expected of a fine musician (no pun intended!)

I would be remiss if I were to omit the fact that I am extremely excited about sharing my knowledge (which is based on a combination of my experiences, education, expertise and employment choices over the past two decades) of this great sport.

Athletically, I have been involved in Flatwater Kayak Racing since 1991. My love of paddling, however, actually commenced three years prior. I can recall being 10 years of age, and going recreational canoeing for the first time at summer camp in the Okanagan in "Beautiful British Columbia". Since that time, some of my athletic highlights have included winning numerous BC Championship and Western Canadian Championship medals. I was a member of the Burnaby Canoe and Kayak Club K-4 crew that won the gold medal in both the K-4 1000m, and K-4 200m (former Canadian Record) events in 1995. In 1998 I won bronze medals at the Canadian Nationals in the Junior Men's K-1 500m and K-1 200m events. These achievements solidified my position as a member of the Canadian Senior National Development Team. In my prime I was a good athlete, perhaps bordering on being a great athlete; nevertheless, I am of the opinion that I never achieved self-actualization. Some may have thought highly of me, but despite my achievements, from a retrospective viewpoint, I suppose I might have made more of an impact in this arena. Perhaps my self-actualization will be achieved as I now meander along on a slightly altered path. It is interesting to note that research has shown that the best athletes do not always have the greatest capacity to impart knowledge, or to coach other athletes. This is, in part, due to the fact that many of the greatest athletes assume far too much with respect to coaching intricacies of minutiae. One might assume that, perhaps, this is a consequence of numerous aspects of a particular sport having come very naturally and easily to them. Obviously, the ability to embrace sound pedagogic technique is a gift unto itself.

Certainly, I am strongly of the opinion that the mighty roots of the unprecedented gifts which have set me apart from many other kayakers are to be found in the formative and formidable years that I spent training and learning on a one-on-one basis under the expert guidance of Dr. Imre Kemecsey. Imre is a former Olympian and world-renowned master coach, and I am both honoured and indebted to have had an ongoing opportunity to learn, define, and refine teachings from much of Imre's vast paddling knowledge. Furthermore, I am also thoroughly delighted to have been used as the "guinea pig" for developing many of the theoretical and practical concepts which will be discussed in subsequent chapters. It should come as no surprise that my years of greatest athletic success transpired when I was working with Imre.

Additionally, I feel that from an academic perspective, I am in a unique position to share much of what I have learned regarding this sport. My post-secondary education commenced at Langara College, in Vancouver, Canada, where I graduated with the Diploma in Coaching & Instruction. Subsequently, I attended the University of British Columbia in Vancouver, where I received the degree of Bachelor of Human Kinetics. A few years later I was admitted to the prestigious Urban Diversity Program at York University in Toronto, where I obtained a Bachelor of Education with a specialization in Physical Education. In addition, I have also commenced a Masters of Education program in Educational Leadership.

Vocationally, I have worked as a coach and assisted in program development at four canoe and kayak clubs throughout Canada; these being the False Creek Racing Canoe Club (Vancouver, BC), the Burnaby Canoe and Kayak Club (Burnaby, BC), the Calgary Canoe Club (Calgary, AB) and the Burloak Canoe Club (Oakville, ON). Career wise, I have chosen a slightly different path, and am in my eighth year of teaching - currently at an inner city high school in Surrey, British Columbia.

As an athlete and coach I have always felt compelled to evaluate three basic premises: 1. What is the ultimate goal with regards to kayak technique and structure/posture? 2. What is the most efficient and effective way to teach various concepts to a variety of kayakers with diverse, and sometimes, unique, needs? 3. Why do some athletes require frequent external error detection cause and correction assistance, while others are able to efficiently and autonomously apply that which has been learned, and work in a self-regulated fashion?

Obviously question #1 can be answered in a far more straightforward manner than the other two, so it is here where I shall divert my attention at this time. Questions #2 and #3 necessitate far more complex and multifaceted responses, and a considerable portion of this book will delve into these issues and concepts in subsequent chapters.

Essentially, how can the athlete minimize resistance on his/her boat while maximizing resistance on the paddle? All things being equal, one would expect that the paddler with a combination of the longest stroke length, and the highest stroke rate, should and would be the fastest. However, there are other factors at play, and therefore, this is not always the case. A powerful engine with a deficient transmission will yield ineffectual results!

There is also much more to *"real kayaking"* than a basic understanding of the four phases of the kayak stroke (i.e. 1. *Catch*, 2. *Pull* or *Power*, 3. *Exit*, and 4. *Recovery* or *Air-Work*). The *catch* is used to accelerate the boat to recover its speed, which has been lost during the *recovery* or *air-work*. During the *pull* or *power* phase, the kayaker must try to establish a smooth running of the boat. In the *Exit* phase, the athlete recovers the blade of the paddle and prepares for the final phase. The *recovery* or *air-work* phase is to enable the paddler to begin the cycle again on the alternate side. Ultimately, and especially in K-1, if the athlete can find a way to maintain a sustained and prolonged pressure on the blade of the paddle at the back end of the stroke, or right before the *exit*, he/she will, in effect, be able to sustain greater boat speed during the *air-work* in preparation for the next *catch*. Rigid, yet flexible, core musculature is vital with regards to preserving this connection throughout the entire stroke. This concept can also be referred to as the *Ice-Cream effect*, which will be explained in ensuing chapters. Once all four phases are put together in succession, the stroke motion should be synchronous. When one phase nears completion, the next phase should transition seamlessly and appear effortless.

In the attempt to paddle the kayak effectively and economically (minimal energy expenditure for a set distance at a particular speed), many other factors must be taken into consideration as well. Kayaking is a sport wherein learning to regulate one's energies and aggression is vital to success. The kayak is, in essence, an extension of one's body (similar in concept to a musical instrument.) How we manipulate our body will impact the run of the kayak, and how we manipulate our kayak will, in turn, cause our body to react and respond in a variety of ways. Kayaking is fundamentally a three-dimensional sport, wherein the body, paddle, and boat move within the *sagittal* (forwards and backwards), *transverse* (rotational), and *frontal* or *coronal* (sideways) planes. Refer to figure 1.1.

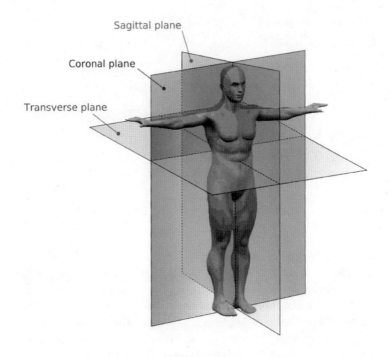

Figure 1.1

Similar to the movement of the human body, the kayak also moves through the water on three axes. This is much as an airplane moves through the air. An airplane can *pitch* or move up and down by using the elevators; it can *yaw* or move sideways by using the rudder; or it can *roll* or rotate by using the ailerons. Refer to Figure 1.2.

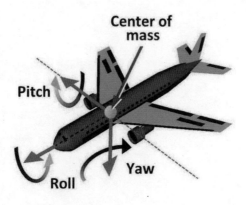

Figure 1.2

In discussing kayak movements, I will respectively refer to *pitch*, *yaw*, and *roll* as *bouncing*, *snaking*, or *rocking* motions. The difference, between the movement of an airplane and a kayak is that with the latter, *for the most part* (there do exist some exceptions), one attempts to minimize these three motions. In other words, if one does not control unwanted motions of the kayak, one will, in turn, create unwanted drag; the resultant effect will be the inevitable slowing of the boat. Furthermore, a kayaker, obviously, does not possess the luxury of engines, and due to the fact that water is 737 times as dense as air, an inability to control unwanted motions will severely and negatively impact boat run. This is not to say that all *bouncing, snaking,* and *rocking* motions are always unwanted, but rather they should emerge as a secondary side-effect of skilful and holistic paddling practices. When focusing on the manner in which the kayak is moving through the water, a proficient coach should be able to identify errors in both technique and structure. Chapter 3 will examine a number of causes and potential remedies for various kayaking errors.

Chapter 2
"Ten Commandments"

At the commencement of developing a framework for this book, I debated as to whether or not I should include a chapter on Imre Kemecsey's *Ten Commandments of Kayaking*. I decided in the affirmative. The "Ten Commandments" have been employed for quite some time, and I am certainly aware that they are definitely **not** of recent origin. Many in the field have become familiar with these over the past twenty years or so. Nevertheless, I choose to include these principles, as I recognize that they still play an important role in comprehending the evolution of newer paddling exercises and structures as these have gradually presented themselves. It is interesting to note that the *Ten Commandments* were never meant to be an all-encompassing kayak technique, although they have been used as such by some coaches and athletes. Rather, these should be viewed as basic exercises, with the knowledge that when practiced sufficiently, they can assist in contributing to a solid, autonomous paddling structure.

The **Ten Commandments of Kayaking** are as follows:

1. *Bent shaft*
2. *Earlier body rotation*
3. *Lock the blade at the catch*
4. *Put more body weight onto the paddle at the catch and during the stroke*
5. *Powerful support in the water before recovery*
6. *Push your shoulder forward from this support*

7. *Do not sit down during the air work*
8. *Suspend the body together with the boat*
9. *Attempt to walk on the surface of the water with the paddle*
10. *There is no waterfall behind you*

Below, I examine each of the "Ten Commandments" on an individual basis, and include a detailed description.

1. Bent shaft: This refers to visualizing that one is capable of bending the shaft of the paddle inwardly toward the body. This is achieved by finding a solid support at the *catch*; this is accomplished by utilizing a good structural tension in the body. As previously stated, I (also redundant) refer to this as the *ice-cream effect*, whereby the ice-cream represents the water and the spoon represents the paddle. As one scoops the ice-cream, the spoon will appear to bend, due to a constant tension. The same must be done with the paddle, continuously and consistently, until its exit from the water.

2. Earlier body rotation: This contends with the fact that everything should be initiated from *the bottom up*. Think about stretching out the stroke-side leg, and *unwinding* the torso, commencing from the hips up to the shoulders.

3. Lock the blade at the catch: This relates to "Commandment" numbers 1 and 2. One should attempt to enter the water with the blade, as cleanly and smoothly as is possible, and lock it as though it is fixed, for a split second, in cement. Try to *glide* past the paddle.

4. Put more body weight onto the paddle at the catch and during the stroke: It is important to note that this does not necessitate leaning on the paddle. Rather, the nervous system must try to find the best way to release body weight from the two contact points in the boat (the heels and buttocks), while maximizing the force that is transferred into the paddle/blade.

5. Powerful support in the water before the recovery: When the blade nears the exit of the *stroke*, the stroke-side hip should start to move forward, thus assisting in the *recovery*, as well as the commencement, of the next stroke (the *whip effect*.) The *support* before *recovery* can be visualized as a second *peak* or *catch*, which will prove to be beneficial toward keeping the speed of the boat speed as high as possible between strokes.

6. Push your shoulder forward from this support: As stated in Commandment #2 (Earlier body rotation), the shoulders should automatically follow the hips due to an *unwinding* of the torso. As the blade exits the water, the stroke-side shoulder should move forward swiftly in order to minimize airtime and begin the next stroke.

7. *Do not sit down during the air work:* This commandment is particularly relevant to K-1. Try to maximize the time that the blade spends in the water, while minimizing the ***air-time*** and/or ***pause.*** Should there be too much ***air-time*** between strokes, the body and the boat will sink down too low into the water. Attempt to be as ***fluid*** as is possible between strokes.

8. *Suspend the body together with the boat:* The paddler should feel as though his/her body, as well as the boat, are both suspended on bungee cords from above. This also relates very closely to the ***do not drag the boat*** philosophy; the mind must find the ideal way to propel the boat forward, in unique partnership with the body. The boat should not follow the paddler, or be *dragged along.*

9. *Attempt to walk on the surface of the water with the paddle:* At higher speeds this should feel similar to a cat-like motion. This is certainly an oxymoron, and deserving of the careful drawing of a very fine line! Although the paddler may be taking deep and powerful strokes, he/she must ultimately find a way to make it appear as though the paddling is occurring on the surface of the water, with the body rising above it. Both the body and the boat should feel extremely buoyant.

10. *There is no waterfall behind you:* Try to have as smooth an ***exit*** and ***recovery*** as is possible, with a minimum of splashing. A great deal of splashing could mean that the paddler is pulling the boat down at the ***exit***, thus reducing its pace. (Newton's Third Law of Motion)

(Kemecsey)

Chapter 3
Bouncing, Snaking, and Rocking Motions – Reasons and Remedies

In Chapter 1, I inspected and illustrated the motion of the kayak upon three planes (this does not include displacement.) In review, these planes are the *sagittal* (forwards and backwards), *transverse* (rotational), and *frontal* or *coronal* (sideways) planes. As a reminder of my attempt to be as straightforward as possible, I will refer to these motions as *bouncing, snaking* and *rocking*, respectively. It is important to note, that no matter how great the attempt, the kayaker will find it virtually impossible to eliminate these motions entirely. However, it is certainly sound practise, and definitely realistic, to minimize these extraneous movements as much as is feasible through the practice of *productive motion remedies*. As coaches and athletes, it is of high importance to convey early on, within the teaching process, that comprehension of Newton's Third Law of Motion is critical to ensuring success (i.e. for every action there is an equal and opposite reaction.) Just, for a moment, visualize the manner in which a basketball or a football will push back against one's hand if it is pressed down into the water. And now, return to the image of paddling a kayak. For the purposes of illustration, a 12 kg K-1 will respond most unfavourably if the paddler merely hacks away at the water in a haphazard fashion.

Bouncing Motion:

The ***bouncing*** motion of the kayak can best be defined as an up and down movement of the bow and stern of the boat, or it can be referred to as a ***seesaw*** motion. The bow of the kayak is naturally inclined to rise during the ***catch***, and to fall during the ***recovery*** or ***air-work***; the movement is vice versa for the stern of the boat.

One cause for the ***bouncing*** is the result of the kayaker moving his/her centre of gravity slightly forward, in an attempt to reach as far as possible by maximizing his/her stroke length. This is a double-edged blade (pun intended!) Although the ***catch*** may well be as far forward as possible, there will be an opposing, negative force with which to contend. By contributing to a greater bounce due to moving the center of gravity forward, the kayaker is, in effect, negating the benefit. There are far more advantageous and beneficial ways to reach with a ***long catch***. At the ***catch***, the athlete will often try to lift himself/herself up off the seat, thus transferring more force into the footboard. As the centre of gravity moves slightly forward beyond the base of support, the bow of the boat will ***submarine***, while the stern of the boat will ascend significantly higher. As the ***catch*** phase ends and the ***pull*** begins, the center of gravity will move backwards, closer to the base of support, once again. At this time, the bow will rise, and the stern will fall again in a ***seesaw*** motion. Although this ***seesaw*** motion happens very quickly, it will hinder the economical forward motion of the boat at the ***catch***. At the commencement of a race, this unwanted motion is most evident; however, once top speed is achieved, the elite paddler should be able to minimize most unintended ***bouncing***.

I can vividly recall that a number of years ago, I often raced against a few particular athletes who did not comprehend the importance of keeping one's center of gravity close to one's base of support, with regards to forward and backward motions. (Sideways motions, where the center of gravity comes outside the base of support, are acceptable.) I still have strong memories as to the method in which these athletes lunged forward during warm-ups (accelerations & starts) to take each ***stroke***; I can but imagine how tiring, taxing, frustrating, and inefficient this must have been. I have definitely witnessed numerous boats ***submarining***, or bouncing up and down, various courses. It is interesting to note that a number of these athletes were actually incredibly strong and fit. There are a few occasions wherein I am able to recall that many of the clubs in my particular geographical region would get together for fitness testing. Some of the athletes connected to these clubs were capable of outperforming me in the weight room, or on various running tests. Fortunately for me, a kayaker does not win paddling races in the weight room ... or on the track!

The looming question, at this point, asks how one can remedy this particular type of *bouncing*. One method is to remove the footboard for an entire workout once a week or more, depending upon the level of the severity of the *bouncing*. By removing the footboard, the athlete's nervous system will be forced to find alternate methods of transferring momentum or energy into the boat, will which not contribute to the common *seesawing* action. Furthermore, coaches can request of their athletes that each do a little exercise, which consists of pressing down into the bottom of the boat or footboard with the heels of his/her feet. With experience and experimentation, I have found that this, too, can be effective at minimizing *bouncing* motions. Moreover, it may be advisable to have the athlete focus on the stern of the boat. Despite the fact that it cannot be seen, he/she must try to sense its location at any given time. After a number of weeks, the kayaker will usually be able to control and correct much of this unintended *bouncing*.

An additional method that coaches may want to employ with their kayakers during practice is the "*Hansen Technique*". In 1998, Imre kemecsey wrote of this technique, "At the 1960 summer Olympics in Rome, Italy, a Danish athlete, Eric Hansen, won the K-1 1000m final with a remarkable new technique. The tall, thin, and not very muscular athlete almost reclined in his boat, while his relatively long paddle propelled/drove him forward on a wider track base. With his wider catch and pull phase he was able to generate a very strong torque. After three or four strokes, however, all bouncing, snaking, and rocking movements were virtually eliminated and his boat moved very smoothly through the water. Subsequently, many athletes tried to copy Hansen's technique with minimal success."

Another explanation for *bouncing* may be due to an inadequate support in the water prior to recovering the blade of the paddle in preparation for the *catch* on the alternate side. Over the years, I have heard many coaches make comments such as, "Do not exit past the hip", "Keep everything up front", or "Harder on the catch". Although a number of these principles may be applicable to team boats, when instructing K-1 paddlers, I believe that these types of critical and ana-lytical comments are unnecessary. A K-1 does not maintain the same degree of momentum between strokes as does a K-2 or K-4; thus it will have the tendency to slow down or *bounce* too much between *strokes* if one is not aware and careful. So... what is the answer? The obvious response is to focus on the back end of the *stroke*. I believe that many coaches advise their athletes to recover their blades at the hip, or even earlier, for a few reasons, these being: 1. Believing this is necessary so as not to pull the boat down into the water, as the blade becomes more horizontal than vertical, as we recover further and further back, and 2. Being unable to recognize the technical and structural differences between paddling a K-1 vs. paddling a K-2 and/or a K-4.

From my own personal paddling experiences, and upon observing elite level K-1 paddlers, I have found that there is no need to focus on the specific point at which the blade exits the water. All athletes are anatomically diverse from one another, and minute subtleties are a fact. As long as the coach takes a holistic approach, the athlete's nervous system will find his/her own individualized point at which the blade should exit and recover. Furthermore, it is not necessary to give the boat (K-1) a huge impulse or catch, provided there is a sufficient *support before recovery (i.e. do not drag the paddle)* at the exit. This type of an exit will ensure that the boat speed drops minimally between strokes, thus reducing bouncing. The exit can even be referred to, or taught, as a *second catch* in the stroke! Some will argue that by *spreading the stroke* or recovering later in the stroke, the boat will be pulled down, thus creating greater resistance by exiting more horizontally. However, if one can *walk* that oh-so-fine line of both swinging and rotating simultaneously during the exit, this potentially negative aspect can and will be avoided. (This concept will be discussed in more detail in subsequent chapters.) Moreover, kayakers should also be taught subtle ways of *pushing or prying* forward, rather than pulling; that is, bringing one's body to the paddle, and not vice-versa.

Snaking Motion:

The *snaking* motion of the kayak can best be defined as a sideways movement of the boat. Due to the fact that the very basics of kayaking involve alternating strokes on opposite sides of the boat, the resultant consequence is that the bow of the kayak has a tendency to have its course altered to the opposite side of the stroke (i.e. the bow will tend to move to the left when paddling on the right, and vice versa.)

Acknowledging the fact that the *snaking* motion of the kayak is a physical result of the basic kayak stroke, one must, nevertheless, examine the methodology for minimizing this movement. This *snaking* motion has the potential to severely inhibit superior boat run by creating a tremendous amount of unwanted drag. Furthermore, the negative consequence to the kayaker is the paddling of added meters, during the attempt to cover a set or pre-determined distance.

There are a variety of causes for superfluous *snaking* motions; fortunately, there are an equal number of methods to remedy these problems. One very basic issue is that the *catch* or the *recovery* may be occurring at a distance too far from the side of the boat. This should be examined first and foremost, and corrected if required (e.g. a *C* boat paddler sometimes turns his/her boat with a big sweeping *C stroke* away from the side of the boat.)

A paddle that is too long for the athlete can also contribute to excess *snaking* motions, as can the commencement of body/torso rotation when the paddle is out of the water (i.e. during the *recovery/ air-work*.) Many of these errors can be corrected by using the same principles that were discussed with regards to *bouncing* (i.e. *pushing* or *prying* forward, instead of pulling.)

One exceptionally effective way to go about neutralizing the *snaking* motion of the boat is to compress (sideways and forwards, or diagonally down and forwards) the opposite hip of the stroke-side, into the side of the boat. This is referred to as the *waterwall* or *waterbed*. Yes... I comprehend that this sounds quite complex and "out there"; however, there is much justification for this approach. Allow me to explain!

One should imagine that he/she is taking a stroke on the left side of the boat. Reflecting on the previous discussion, the kayak's bow will naturally move slightly to the right, thus creating excess drag. Now imagine that the kayaker takes that same stroke, but this time *counterbalancing* is employed by utilizing the lower body through the method of compressing the opposite hip into the side of the boat. It is no secret that, as a result of the paddler's own actions, that element which is outside the kayak ... water ... will take on the capacity to be a best friend or a worst enemy! In effect, there is a wall of water (*waterwall*) that is constantly pushing against the side of the boat, and vice versa, thus assisting with displacement and keeping the kayak afloat (*waterbed*). Now... reconsider (found at the commencement of this chapter) Newton's Third Law of Motion, "For every action there is an equal and opposite reaction." It should soon become obvious (especially with a little practise!) that if the kayaker is (or becomes!) competent in compressing the opposite side (right side) of the boat into the **waterwall**, there will be an opposite reaction or action which will consist of the water pushing upon the boat to the left, thereby **equalizing the torque**. On a personal level, I initially had some difficulty comprehending and integrating this process into my kayaking technique, therefore I am very aware of the complexity of issues involved. A skilful manipulation of this situation, which may assist some paddlers, is to focus primarily on the stroke-side hip (left hip), and to note that it is rotating backwards and somewhat sideways. As one becomes aware of this, it will soon become obvious that the right hip cannot do anything other than to compress forward and sideways into the **waterwall**. Additionally, a slight rotation of the legs to the stroke-side can also be of tremendous assistance (this will be discussed in much greater detail when I advise about **rocking**.) As well, it is also possible to **twist** the bow of the boat into the direction of the stroke-side, thus assisting to eliminate the **snaking** motion.

The **wet soap effect** is also of considerable significance as a metaphor to apply during visualization. The comparison can be made that just as a wet bar of soap will slip out of one's hand under the application of too much pressure, it is the stroke side-blade collectively with the effect of the (opposite) **waterwall** against the boat, that work in unison to compress the boat forward in a straight line. At this point, it should be noted that these concepts and techniques provide much information as to the overall truth that all aspects of paddling are interdependent upon one-another; very few aspects of paddling work in isolation. Again, I remind you that the whole is greater than the sum of its parts.

An extremely effective pedagogy for many of these concepts (if not all!) is the **Power Circles**, created by Imre Kemecsey. These will be discussed in great detail in Chapter 5.

Rocking Motion:

The **rocking** motion of the kayak can be circumscribed as the submerging of one side of the boat, while the other side rises concurrently. For example, if the paddler takes a stroke on the left, he/she will naturally have a tendency to tilt the boat to the right, and vice versa – this is an inclination which is incorrect, and practice is important to remedy this problem.

It is normal for a novice paddler to rock the boat away from the stroke-side. This action/reaction occurs subconsciously for a variety of reasons. Being new to the sport, the paddler will usually feel more stable in the boat by leaning away from the stroke-side. Furthermore, this may also occur due to the fatigue of the spinal erector and gluteus muscles. Unfortunately, if one allows his/her boat to lean to the opposite side of the stroke, maximal power transmission will not occur, and a strong potential connection will be forfeited.

The *rocking* motion of the kayak can become even more counterproductive should the athlete not transfer his/her weight in an appropriate manner throughout the blade and the boat. Ultimately, the paddler must discover the most effective way in which to diminish his/her weight in the boat, and consequently apply this load to the paddle. In an attempt at clarification, one might ask, "In what manner can one minimize the resistance on the boat, and maximize it on the blade of the paddle?"

When examining elite level kayakers (particularly those in K-1), it becomes remarkably apparent that these paddlers consistently apply their body weight toward the stroke-side. It should be noted that there is a major difference between leaning to the stroke-side, and applying some body weight to the stroke side. In fact, the great paddler is actually able to **walk a fine line** by swinging and leaning away from the stroke while concurrently applying body weight to the stroke side. The reader may, at this juncture, be wondering how this is feasible. Allow me to assure you that this practice is definitely attainable. As long as the paddler is able to find a solid, fixed point in the water and **grab it** with his/her blade, he/she can simultaneously rotate the legs slightly toward the stroke-side, while leaning the boat toward the stroke-side, effectually creating momentum with a vigorous upper body rotation and swing away from the **centre line**, toward the support or opposite side. Over the years, I have been witness to coaches uttering numerous directives with which I do not agree. One such example is, "Lean on the paddle." I am strongly of the opinion that such a statement has the potential to be very misleading. If the kayaker were truly to *lean on the paddle*, he/she would be swimming! **Dynamic Stability** (support due to motion) is crucial in this circumstance.

Summarily, in an attempt to eliminate the *rocking* motion, the kayaker should lean the boat to the stroke-side for as long as the blade is in the water. This is a sustained lean that works in unison with the stroke-side leg. Only upon the completion of the stroke (*exit*) should the paddler begin the transition to leaning the boat to the opposite side. I highly recommend *figure eights* and *circles* as remarkable drills with which to assist the athlete in this area. (Refer to Chapter 7 – Skills & Drills)

Chapter 4
Tensegrity (Tensional Integrity)

The concept of *Tensegrity* or *tensional integrity* introduces the kayaker to an inter-connection and inter-reliance of relevant anatomy; this is attained through the use of agonist (prime mover) and antagonist (stabilizer) muscle groups, in relation as to how they pull on and affect the skeleton. In order to create movement, the body needs to create *tension* (pull) through the muscles and tendons, as well as *compression* (push) through the bones. Neither can exist in isolation! Ultimately, if these tensions and compressions are in equilibrium, the tensions will meet at a compression point and *balance each other out*, thus generating momentum. Although, in the abstract, this may appear as if it is a very complicated skill to master, in reality, it can be taught to athletes through the pedagogical concept of the five *Power Circles*, which will be discussed in much greater depth in Chapter 5.

The *Tensegrity* concept can be useful for the kayaker as a significant means for envisioning and comprehending the inter-relationships between the body, boat, paddle, and the water. By its very nature, kayaking necessitates that the athlete maintains stability on an unstable platform (the kayak), while alternating strokes on opposite sides. Furthermore, the athlete must also apply maximum force to the paddle at a maximum stroke rate. This is obviously no easy feat; the kayaker is called upon to deal with mental, technical, tactical, physiological, and environmental factors simultaneously.

One of the most important criterions, which distinguishes the elite athlete from the novice, is the comprehension, whether it be conscious or unconscious, that different phases in the stroke require varying amounts of rigidity at different points in the stroke. The elite paddler also has a far greater capacity to adapt to changes required by an open environment; this may be, in part, due to nervous system adaptations. In contrast, the abilities of the novice will embody varying degrees of a very rigid, inadaptable structure, and he/she will thus expend unnecessary energy. In essence, the novice paddler will work against the water, whereas the experienced athlete will work with the water in a constant and consistent attempt to use it to his/her advantage. In other words, the elite athlete has mastered the oxymoron of controlling his/her aggression while still relaxing! Ultimately, the elite paddler is keenly aware of his or her boat run, and is able to minimize unwanted side effect motions of the boat, often described as *chewing gum paddling*.

Through the utilization of appropriate imagery and/or metaphors, it is possible for a kayaker to realize and benefit from the principles of the *tensegrity* approach, whether consciously acknowledged or not. Of course, no two athletes learn in exactly the same manner and style, and therefore, no two athletes should be coached using the "cookie cutter" approach. The pedagogical challenge is to find a way for the athlete to take responsibility for the learning process and the mastery of various concepts by creating his or her own unique kayaking *picture*. Upon first learning these concepts (many of which I shall be discussing in later chapters), I recall being frustrated and discontented at times; this was obviously due to the many directions being give to me. Nevertheless, I had tremendous faith and trust in my coach's abilities; I never relinquished the hope of eventually creating the best possible holistic mental picture for myself. There were those times when many of the drills that I attempted seemed to be somewhat counterproductive to my technique. Nevertheless, I was well aware that these temporary setbacks were due to unlearning bad habits, and that this would necessitate spending the time necessary in relearning various new concepts and techniques. I had an intense belief that the time would eventually come when everything would feel really comfortable and just *click* into place for me. I encourage the kayaker to utilize various mental pictures which were created by both Imre and me, being certain all the while that these images make sense, as he/she incorporates them into a paddling mindset.

Obviously, over time, and with experience in this methodology, one should feel free to individually employ modifications to that which has been said, and will be discussed, in ensuing chapters.

The *tensegrity* concept examines nothing in isolation. In essence, it allows for the visualization and creation at a high level, yet in a relatively simplistic manner, for an athlete to quickly conceptualize his/her own paddling skills. Ultimately, the paddler will be prompted into a modus operandi wherein a superior level of awareness will be acquired with regards as to how his/her body works in unison with the boat, paddle, and the water. In other words, the kayaker will ultimately grasp the importance of the manner in which tension lines interact with compression points during the stroke.

Throughout the kayak stroke, the efficient paddler will learn to generate compression points inside the body through the junction of at least two tension lines; as a result, enormous forces will automatically be transferred. Imaginary tension lines within the athlete's body allow for concentration on the function of only those muscles in close proximity to the tension lines (i.e. *Power Circles*.) To be succinct, compression occurs when at least two tensions converge. For instance, a paddler's top hand, during the stroke, acts as a compression point inside the structure, as a result of tension lines converging on a particular point from synchronized compression points. The top hand compression occurs in conjunction with the opposite hip compressing against the side of the boat, while the opposite buttock cheek is moving backwards, and the hip-side leg/foot is compressing against the footboard. (Refer to figures 4.1 and 4.2)

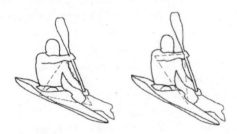

Figure 4.1   Figure 4.2

It is interesting to note that as soon as one applies force to this structure, the tension lines and compression points are able to move to a certain extent; however, the fundamental characteristics of the structure or technique do not, and should not, change in a significant manner. Ultimately, the competent athlete should be able to lock into an autonomous state of flow. Eventually, the athlete's nervous system will take over by being both proactive and reactive in terms of creating an autonomous technical and structural balance in the system. Obviously, this will have a distinct look and feel from one kayaker to another, as such additional factors as height, weight, length of limbs, type of equipment being used, etc. must be given due consideration.

At this juncture, I find it incumbent upon myself to stress, yet again, the importance of the *tensegrity* concept. When unfamiliar with this, I am well aware that it might appear to be very complex and impractical. Nevertheless, the reality is that it is not particularly complicated or elaborate. This concept can and will assist kayakers to create a holistic and all-encompassing mental picture, which will emerge as a strong basis for error detection, cause, and correction.

Some coaches may find it helpful to explain the following *tightrope* analogy to their kayakers. A tightrope walker is required to walk on an extremely tight cable, high above the ground. In his/her hands, this athlete holds a long rod or stick, while practising or performing. In essence, one is performing a similar action in the kayak. The paddler is required to balance in the kayak, while alternating sides in succession. The *motor* is, in effect, the twisting or swinging of the trunk of the body. In accomplishing this momentum, one is actually losing his/her balance temporarily. Balance is recovered due to a precise entry of the blade at the *catch*. There is strong evidence of this momentary loss of balance when looking at the results of paddlers who break their paddle or blade due to a tremendous amount of force ... these athletes often end up swimming!!!

In biomechanical terms, kayaking stability will increase as one's center of gravity is lowered, with the center of gravity being moved as close to the base of support as possible. However, in due course, it is crucial that the paddler learns to temporarily move his or her center of gravity away from the base of support in order to generate a greater impulse/torque, and subsequently, greater velocity with minimal effort.

One final thought that I would like to share at this time regarding the *tensegrity* concept is in comparing it to a suspension bridge. Do not misunderstand! When I was first introduced to this analogy by my coach, Dr. Imre Kemecsey, I probably had the same look on my face as you do at this very moment! I thought to myself, "What does a bridge have to do with kayak structure and technique?" Nevertheless, I heard him out, and I hope you will do the same for me. Although there is obviously a fundamental difference in that a bridge is a static structure, and a kayaker is moving dynamically, there are still some significant similarities. As the reader will recall, I discussed that in kayaking, tensions meet at compression points and balance each other out. The same is true for the suspension bridge. (See figure 4.3)

(caption Figure 4.3)

The photograph above is of the Alex Fraser Bridge, which is part of highway 91, east of Vancouver, British Columbia, Canada. This suspension bridge has two main concrete structures or towers, where all the cables or tensions converge. On the opposite side of the concrete towers there are also cables or tensions that converge, thereby creating an opposite tension (in effect, a compression in comparison to the opposite side.) If not for these cables, this bridge would be totally lacking in the capacity to stand on its own. Even if the bridge had cables (or tensions) on only one side of the concrete towers, it would eventually fail. By means of comparison, these same principles apply in creating a well- balanced structure in kayaking. The tensions must meet at a compression point in order to balance out one another. While it is true that the bridge could be operational with more towers for each set of cables, this is not necessary. In fact, it could be considered overkill. In the kayak, overkill is a possibility as well. In summation, I reiterate that paddling a kayak in a highly effective manner involves a very fine balance between the body, the paddle, the boat, and perhaps, most importantly, the water! An over emphasis or over reliance on physiological or muscular factors is all too common, and has the potential to be counterproductive.

(Kemecsey)

Chapter 5
Five Power Circles

Feeling most fortunate both to have learned about, and to have had much opportunity to diligently practise the Five *Power Circles*, I am strongly of the opinion that the ability and facility to conjure up these mental images are the holistic backbone of kayak structure and technique. This relatively new way of thinking is the future of paddling, and has the ability to create a solid foundation from which to improve upon. That which I find so exciting and interesting about the *power circles* are their pedagogical advantages. There is very little need to analyze athletes in a critical fashion; thus, as a most positive consequence, the vast majority of coaching feedback will be in the form of constructive reinforcement. These *five power circles*, developed by Dr. Imre Kemecsey, commence in a most straightforward manner, and gradually compound upon one another in order of difficulty. Should the paddler be motivated to learn these beneficial *circles*, it will be possible, eventually, to perform all *five power circles* in a simultaneous manner. The final culmination is the attainment of the inordinate balance gained as a result of all the *power circles'* tensions and compressions working in unison; this is termed the *Wishbone Effect*. At this point, whether the athlete is consciously aware or not, he/she will be automatically employing many of the principles of counterbalancing and *tensegrity (tensional integrity.)*

As coaches, it is essential to keep the following concepts in mind while teaching the *five power circles*:

1. The goal is to create a well balanced structure wherein the tensions meeting at compression points have the effect of balancing each other out.

2. Compression occurs when at least two tensions converge.

3. *Power Circles* one, two, and three deal primarily with dynamic body positions, whereas *power circles* four and five incorporate a greater connection between the body and the boat.

4. All *power circles* incorporate a *power center* that changes slightly throughout the stroke. Furthermore, all *power circles* have a *common power center*.

5. Fundamentally speaking, compressions usually relate to a *push*, and tensions usually relate to a *pull (Tensegrity.)*

It is important to note that it is unnecessary to talk to the paddler about the *final form* of the kayak structure. Rather, the coach should attempt to focus on sensory learning methods, which will help all paddlers regardless of discipline (Flatwater, Surfski, etc.)

Power Circles can and should be viewed as a series of forces. Below, are concise descriptions that may assist the paddler in focusing on the crucial aspects of these *circles*. Diagrams are also presented for each *power circle*, with the express intent to aid the athlete with the sensation of the transmission of forces or power lines. More detailed descriptions have also been included.

<u>Circle #1:</u> This *circle* encourages the paddler to focus on forces travelling between the pulling-side hand, to the pulling-side footboard, to the pulling-side hip, to the pulling-side shoulder, and back to the hand. This forms a circle that changes shape throughout the stroke, but the force stays intact throughout the pulling phase of the stroke. This is referred to as the *Vertical Hula-Hoop.*

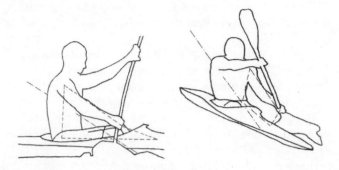

PC #1

>> Foot board on the pulling side >> straightening, contracting leg >> hip >> trunk muscles on the pulling side >> pulling arm, hand >> back to the foot board on the pulling side

Compression: Contracting leg >> hip >> trunk on the stroke side

Tension: Stroke side arm

Circle #2: This *circle* focuses on the upper body connection of the shoulders and arms with the paddle. This is described as the *Horizontal Hula-Hoop.*

PC #2

>> Pulling arm, hand >> shoulder on the pulling side >> shoulder on the support side >> supporting arm, hand >> through the shaft to the pulling hand

Compression: Shoulder on the stroke side >> shoulder on the support side >> arm on the support side

Tension: Stroke side arm

Circle #3: This *circle* focuses on the lower body. This can be imaged as the **Powerful Bicycle**. One should contemplate being earlier with the legwork, while releasing weight from the support-side buttock.

PC #3
>> Footboard on the stroke side >> straightening, contracting leg >> hip on the stroke side >> hip on the support side >> back to the foot board on the pulling side
Compression: Straightening and contracting leg >> hip on the stroke side
>> Hip on the support side >> back to the foot board on the stroke side
Tension: Support side leg/foot pulling on the support side foot strap/ foot bar

Circle #4: This *circle* focuses on the connection from the pulling-side blade to the opposite hip. This circle can also be referred to as the **Inverted V**, as the line of power on the stroke-side blade up the arm to the stroke-side shoulder, is coupled with the compression of the opposite hip. Upon observation, one will note that these power lines do indeed follow and form an upside-down V relationship.

PC #4
>> Blade fixed in the water >> shoulder on the stroke side >> hip on the support side >> back to the blade fixed in the water
Compression: Shoulder on the stroke side >> hip on the support side >> back to blade in the water
Tension: Blade in the water >> shoulder on the stroke side

Circle #5: This *circle* is the most complex and encompasses almost the entire body. It deals with the connection from the stroke side leg/hip to the support side upper body/arm.

PC #5
>> Foot board on the stroke side >> straightening and contracting leg >> hip on the stroke side >> shoulder on the support side >> support side arm/hand >> back to the foot board on the stroke side
Compression: Foot board on the stroke side >> straightening and contracting leg >> hip on the stroke side >> shoulder on the support side >> support side arm/hand >> "back" to the foot board on the stroke side.
Tension: *none in this power circle*

Power Circles:

Detailed Descriptions:

***Power Circle* #1**: This *circle* is initiated from the stroke-side foot pushing against the footboard. The reacting force (from foot-board to foot) is transferred toward the stroke-side hip. The stroke-side hip pushes against the seat. From the seat, the motion is transferred up the torso to the *locked* stroke-side shoulder, and then to the stroke-side hand, which pulls against the paddle. The pulling force from the hand, coupled with lower body tension and pressure on the foot-board, act to propel the boat forward. This *circle* becomes complete when the force from the stroke-side hand to the paddle is transferred back to the foot pressing on the foot-board. (Think of PC #1 as taking place on one side of the body.)

***Power Circle* #2**: In this *circle* the lower hand initiates the compression against the paddle and the resulting force is transferred through the arm to the stroke-side shoulder. As the shoulder moves backwards, the opposite shoulder moves forwards. Both shoulders work as a unit to transfer force from the lower hand to the upper hand. The shoulders must act in unison, held in a firm position, in order to accomplish an effective transfer of force. The upper hand now pushes against the shaft, which transfers force to the stroke-side hand to complete the circle. (Think of PC #2 as being about *body rotation*.)

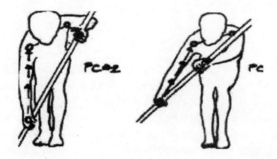

__Power Circle__ #3: The ***powerful bicycle*** is initiated by pressing the foot against the foot-board. The resulting force moves toward the stroke-side hip. The hip is compressing against the seat. These combined forces are transferred to the opposite hip, which plays an important role in this ***power circle.*** The opposite hip presses sideways against the boat, which counteracts the turning effect of the paddle stroke. This positively affects the boat in its running a straight course. Once the resulting force from the hip compression is transferred back to the stroke-side foot, this circle is complete. (Think of PC #3 as *leg work.*)

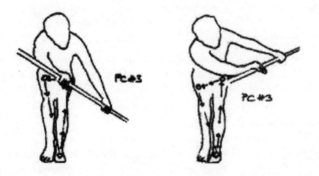

__Power Circle__ #4: The blade's compression against the water initiates force which is transferred to the stroke-side shoulder. That force is then transferred to the opposite hip. The opposite hip pushes against the side of the boat opposite to the stroke-side. The resulting force from the opposite hip is transferred back to the pivot point of the blade in the water to complete this circle. (Think of PC #4 as being about the *shoulder to hip swing*.)

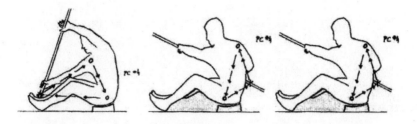

Power Circle #5: The final and most difficult **power circle** to master uses the compression of the stroke-side foot against the foot-board to transfer force to the stroke-side hip. The stroke-side hip then pushes against the seat, and the combined forces from the foot and hip are transferred to the opposite pushing- side shoulder. The shoulder and arm then compress the hand against the paddle. Force is transferred back to the foot to complete the **circle**. (Think of PC #5 as being about the *body swing*, with firm imaginary rods crossing the frame or torso.)

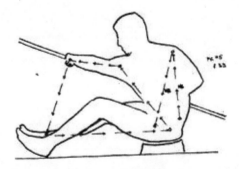

It must be noted that the **power circles** can and should be thought of as the basic structural foundation of kayaking. Although they are not representative of the entire picture of the technique of this sport, nevertheless, once the athlete has developed an understanding of these, with an ability to physically execute them, many other technical and structural factors may gradually be added to this foundation. Initially, these are complex; personally, I would be averse to teaching all the **power circles** at the same time. The attempt to do this may cause the athlete to experience mental overload and frustration. One useful strategy that coaches may want to employ is to encourage the paddler to focus only unilaterally at first (one side at a time.) For example, the kayaker could work on the compression of the left leg and right arm during *power circle* #5. Later, he/she could focus on the compression of the right leg and the left arm. Finally, the athlete can try putting it all together, working bilaterally (on both sides.) Subsequently, sooner or later, the coach should be able to call out one or more numbers from one through five, and the athlete should be able to proactively or reactively modify his/her technique and structure for the better.

In due course, the nervous system of the competent kayaker should be able to execute the *wishbone effect* by finding the most efficient point/position in the stroke, and maintaining it for as long as the blade is in the water. This will serve to maximize the benefits of the *kinetic chain*. Additionally, the paddler may be able to achieve the *wishbone effect* by finding the *Common Power Center*, situated precisely where the power lines of *power circles* #4 and #5 cross in an *X pattern* within the torso. (Chapter 6, #12)

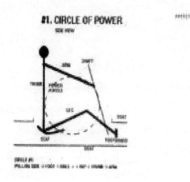

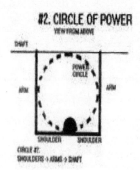

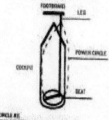

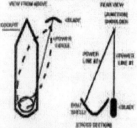

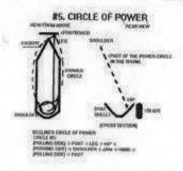

(Kemecsey)

Photographs

Training on Burnaby Lake – Burnaby, British Columbia (1998)

Premier's Athletic Award – Vancouver, British Columbia (1999)
(With Minister of Sport Ian Waddell and Premier Glen Clark)

K4 1000 Meters – Canadian National Championships
– Welland, Ontario (Lane 5) (1995)

K1 500 Meters – Canadian National Championships
– Whistler, British Columbia (1998)

K1 500 Meters – Canadian National Championships
– Whistler, British Columbia (1998)

Western Canadian Championships – Calgary, Alberta (2001)

K1 200 Meters Western Canadian Champion
– Calgary, Alberta (2001)

K1 200 Meters – Canada Day Regatta – Regina, Saskatchewan (2001)

Imre Kemecsey –Conducting a Coaching Presentation (2010)

K2 500 Meters – Pacific Cup Regatta –
Maple Ridge, British Columbia (2010)

K1 10,000 Meters – Pitt Meadows, British Columbia (2011)

Practicing a *Start* on Burnaby Lake (2011)

A Prime Example of *Leaning the Boat
toward the Stroke-Side* (2011)

Rest Time!!! (2011)

Chapter 6
Complementary Structural and Technical Concepts

Assuming that the athlete has reached a level wherein he/she has grasped many of the ideas that have been discussed in previous chapters, it will, subsequently, be valuable to further refine, build upon, and solidify these ideas through the use of *complementary structural and technical concepts*. Many of the following paragraphs in this chapter pertain to the ideal *holistic* kayak structure and technique. At times I will compare and contrast various common mental pictures or metaphors, which encompass specific imaging of the water, boat, paddle, and/or body in order to create an all-encompassing vision, guided by positive reinforcement/affirmation concepts. Furthermore, I have made an effort to structure the following interdependent concepts in an order based on the premise that the kayak stroke is initiated from the *bottom up.*

1) *Lean the Boat to the Stroke-Side:* This concept has previously been discussed in Chapter 3. Nevertheless, it retains such importance, and is so vitally necessary in the attempt to execute proper boat run, that it is my strong contention that it should be touched upon briefly yet again. Upon examining videos of the most outstanding kayakers in the world, it is obvious that they are *leaning their boats to the stroke-side*. Perhaps these athletes do this naturally, or perhaps it has been taught. Nevertheless, for the majority of paddlers who keep the boat totally centered, or those who lean their boat away from the stroke-side, I challenge them to try paddling both away from the stroke-side and towards the stroke-side. I am certain that in a very short period of time, these kayakers will come to the realization that the latter method is certainly the way to go. Eventually, leaning away from the stroke-side will seem very unnatural and foreign. At this point, a much more powerful connection will be evident. It should also be noted that if the athlete is working with *powerful legwork*, and out-stretching the stroke-side leg (in the correct sequence), the boat will automatically and consequently lean to the stroke-side. It should be clearly noted that this is NOT a forced movement, but rather the boat will lean to the stroke-side as a result of powerful legwork, and proper torso rotation/swing. One way to prove the effectiveness of leaning towards the stroke-side is to hold onto the dock while first leaning away from the stroke-side, and then leaning toward the stroke side, all the while pumping the legs. The kayaker will notice very quickly that when leaning away from the stroke-side leg, it is almost impossible to maximize the leg drive and rotation; when leaning toward the stroke-side, maximal transfer of power is attained.

2) *Earlier Leg:* This concept relates to the paddler's attempt, as much as possible, to initiate the whole stroke by *driving down* the stroke-side leg (knee extension). In theory, a potent visual concept is to imagine that one is breaking the footboard. Obviously, in reality this will not occur; however, this is one method to allow for the creation of a vivid mental image. I am fully aware that this notion is controversial and that many coaches teach their athletes to hold off on the *leg drive*, and to begin the *catch* first. Nevertheless, based on both the practical research that I have conducted, as well as on my observations of numerous high-level paddlers, I believe that the legs must come first, and that everything should be initiated from the bottom up. This is especially crucial for the 200 meter race, as this practice allows one to force the stroke rate to an increased level.

3) *Shaky Legs:* This concept relates very closely to #2 (Earlier Leg), in that it pertains to driving the foot into the footboard while keeping a sustained pressure against it. It is not adequate merely to just kick it, but rather the *tensegrity (tensional integrity)* or connection with the footboard must remain until the blade of the paddle exits the water. My reasoning for terming this *Shaky Legs* is due to the physiological

fact that at high intensities (racing), the legs will actually start to *twitch* or *shake*. It is a temporary or instantaneous isometric muscle action. If done correctly, it is quite conceivable for the leg muscles to fatigue prior to any others in the body! It may prove advantageous for a kayaker to get into the habit of doing leg-strengthening exercises at a gym, as all too often there is an unrecognized tendency for the legs to be neglected.

4) *Overlapping Knees:* This concept concerns itself with utilizing the knees for counterbalance. While the paddler is using his/her legs during the stroke, he/she must attempt to counterbalance with the knees; this is best achieved by overlapping them. For example, taking into account that this is a very subtle motion, as the paddler takes a stroke (or just prior to the stroke) on the left side, he/she should try to rotate and compress the right support leg/knee to the stroke-side while counter-compressing the left leg/knee a little under the right side support leg/knee, and vice versa. Furthermore, as the paddler creates a compression with the stroke-side leg on the footboard, he or she should simultaneously pull vigorously and create a strong opposing tension on the footstrap by using the support-side leg. This is a form of counterbalance, and will in effect minimize unwanted snaking motions, as well as assist in creating balance in the structure.

5) *Twist the Boat:* As most are aware, when one takes a stroke on the left side, the boat inclines itself to turn to the right, and vice versa. Based on the aforementioned concept, ***overlapping knees***, if the athlete does this correctly, he or she can actually equalize the *snaking* torque that is created by the stroke. One can prove this to oneself by attempting the following exercise. If the kayaker sits in his/her boat holding onto the dock, and commences with the leg motion (while overlapping the knees), the bow of the boat will *snake* slightly towards the stroke-side. This is significant, because when paddling energetically, one will obviously employ his/her legs in a more vigorous fashion than when not. In essence, he/she will be able to counter much of the negative *snaking* torque by twisting the bow of the boat into the *waterwall* on the stroke-side.

6) *RipStik:* Over the past few years, I have had the opportunity of observing many new types of skateboards (Ripstick) that twist or rotate in the middle. This skateboard allows the *skater* to effectively speed up, or even go uphill, while never taking his/her feet off the board; it basically eliminates the necessity to push off from the ground. This forward momentum is generated entirely from a powerful sideways motion. This concept is applicable for kayaking in that the paddler must rotate his/her legs towards the **stroke-side**, while simultaneously compressing against the **waterwall** on the **support-side** or opposite hip side. If done correctly, the boat should run extremely efficiently and smoothly because this is a major aspect of the real **diagonal connection.**

7) **Tube of Toothpaste:** This concept is very similar to the RipStik idea discussed above; nevertheless, this analogy may help to further simplify and solidify this notion. One should imagine that he/she is holding a tube of toothpaste in a horizontal manner with both hands, and is twisting the tube back and forth in the attempt to squeeze out the toothpaste. In the kayak, the knees and legs can be considered to be one end of the toothpaste tube on the stroke-side, and the hips and buttocks are the other end of the toothpaste tube on the support-side. These two points should be twisting away from each other during each and every stroke.

8) **Edge the Boat:** This concept has gained and garnered its credence based on trial and error, as well as by observing water-skiers, and fish. Although a water-skier is towed by a motorboat, he/she still maintains the ability to increase his/her instantaneous speed by creating a solid support in the water through leaning or edging into the water. A water skier does NOT increase his or her momentum by twisting the ankles/feet; rather he/she leans, just as a kayaker must lean the boat toward the stroke-side. The barracuda, one of the fastest fish known to mankind, is a master of **edging**, and also employs a similar concept which enables it to accelerate incredibly quickly. The barracuda does not use its fins and tail to accelerate quickly; rather, it pushes sideways into the water in an extremely precise and accurate manner (i.e. sideways and diagonally back.) As a kayaker, one must come to the realization that the paddles' blades (fins and tail) alone are not sufficient to propel the boat forward at an elite level or speed. (Chapter 3 – **Snaking** Motions – the **Waterwall** and the **Wet Soap Effect**, for additional concepts that relate to this idea)

9) Create a *Big C:* The ***Big C*** is very similar in concept to the #1 and #5 ***power circles.*** However, in terms of imagery, it creates yet another visual picture for the paddler. The power is initiated on the footboard, and transfers up through the foot, to the leg, to the hip, through the torso, through the shoulder, into the arm, and finally into the support-side pushing hand. The reason for it being called the ***Big C*** is because the power is transferred upwardly through the body in the shape of the letter "C".

10)*Create a Sideways C:* There are two ***Sideways C's,*** and these are evident only on the stroke-side. When the kayaker counterbalances throughout the duration of the stroke, he/she should be creating a slight ***C*** with his/her body, which should be evident from the front or (and???) the back. As the paddler leans the boat to the stroke-side, the legs should also rotate and lean toward that side. At the same time, the middle of the spine should have a slight inward bend in it, and the upper body should be swinging to create temporary momentum, by moving the centre of gravity outside of the base of support (toward the support-side.) Finally, the head and cervical vertebrae (upper spine) should be leaning slightly back towards the stroke-side, and the top of the ***C*** should be considered as the middle of the paddle shaft. ***Figure 8's*** and ***circles*** practice will help greatly with learning this concept. (Chapter 7 – Skills and Drills)

11) *Imagine the Eiffel Tower:* This is yet another mental picture that can prove beneficial in helping to explain the manner in which the centre of gravity can exist and function effectively, at least temporarily, outside of the base of support. One should attempt to create the mental image that one side of the Eiffel Tower is the stroke-side blade, and the other side of the Tower is (are??? not sure) the contact points in the boat, these being the buttocks, and the heels. It will soon become evident that the bend in the tower is very similar to the body of the kayaker, in that the torso and hips, etc. should maintain a bend as well. This will evolve and alter throughout the stroke; nevertheless, the principals are always the same. The paddler should consider the ***diagonal line of force*** going up from the stroke-side blade, across the back, to the opposite shoulder/hand. (Chapter 4 – ***Tensegrity*** Concept)

12) *Twist and Rotate the X:* This concept deals with the image that there is an X planted in the ground, and that the top of the X is being pulled so that it will rotate and swing around itself. The top of this X can be considered to be the shoulders, whereas the bottom of the X represents the hips. This concept is similar to many of the others of which I speak; nevertheless, it presents to coaches, elitist kayakers, and novice paddlers alike yet one more mental picture that may prove to be useful within the grand scheme of high-level performance.

13) *Create the Imaginary Connection between Opposite Shoulder and Stroke-Side Hip:* When taking a stroke on the left, think about the right side shoulder as having an imaginary connection, wherein it is compressing towards the left side hip, and vice versa. This concept will assist greatly with sustaining an efficient momentum.

14) *Visualize the Momentum of a Penguin:* As a penguin walks, its waddle from side to side is most noticeable. I was instructed that a penguin moves in this manner due to incredible efficiency. It is able to utilize the momentum generated from the last step to assist with successive steps. It is possible to apply this concept to kayaking as well. As one takes a stroke, it is a given that muscular energy is used; nevertheless, it is possible to assist the muscles (counterbalancing) and conserve some energy by combining a swing and a lean with the upper body, thus mimicking the waddling penguin! Although this is by no means perpetual motion, I believe that it is an infinitesimal step in that direction, and minute changes can ultimately make a substantial difference. As an exercise, coaches might advise a kayaker to attempt to paddle in a penguin-like fashion. (Potato Sack Drill in Chapter 7 – Skills and Drills)

15) *Create an Image of Pole Vaulting:* The employment of this concept, in terms of mental imagery, has proven itself to be highly effective for kayakers. In this exercise, the paddler imagines that he/she is *pole vaulting* by planting his/her paddle in a similar manner to planting a pole, thus creating a bend in the paddle (potential energy) from which to *launch* the boat and body forward at the *exit* (kinetic energy.) This concept has a resemblance to **Lock the Blade and Glide.**

16) *Visualize a Full Swing:* This exercise is very similar in conceptualization to the **Penguin** (#14). The paddler should imagine that there is a bungee cord attached to each hip and shoulder from the front (four in total.) As a stroke is initiated on the left side, the attempt should be made to stretch out these bungee cords as much as possible, for the entire duration of the stroke. Once the stroke has been completed, the identical concept should be practiced on the right side; this should proceed in a successive manner.

17) *Attempt a Second Catch:* This concept is especially significant when paddling a K-1, and probably somewhat less significant in K-2s and K-4s. Just before the exit of the stroke, the paddler should try to create a second impulse, and aim to **spread the stroke**, thus not allowing the boat to slow down significantly during the **recovery** or **air-work**. My personal opinion is that this is one of the most pertinent differences between paddling a K-1 versus a K-2 or K-4. All things being equal, a K-1 will have a slower stroke rate, a slower speed (water will be moving slower past the boat), and less potential for creating power and speed. It is therefore crucial that the entire pull or power phase of the stroke is maximized while the blades of the paddle are in the water. A powerful catch alone is not adequate.

18) *Visualize the Ice-Cream Effect:* This analogy provides the kayaker with yet another way in which to visualize the **second catch**. The paddler should create a mental picture whereby the paddle is the spoon, and the water is the ice-cream! As the ice-cream is being scooped, the spoon should bend; so too should the shaft of the paddle in the water. (Not recommended if one is feeling hungry!) This is completely opposed to the **Fred Flintstone Effect**, where one just spins out of control, revving the stroke rate too high prior to feeling a true connection. Those who are familiar with the cartoon series, "The Flintstones", will note that Fred moves his legs at a very fast pace at first, without getting anywhere. This is a prime example of that which we do not wish to see in kayaking! This can also be compared to driving a car and never shifting out of first gear.

19) *Envision the Use of More Deltoid & Triceps and Less Biceps:* This concept deals with very subtle and miniscule details. Nevertheless, if the athlete is swinging properly and precisely, it should occur, almost as a natural cause and effect (and vice versa), that the athlete will recover the blade at the back of the stroke by using less elbow flexion in exchange for more shoulder extension. This type of practice will further ensure that the paddler is using the larger back musculature while minimizing the exertion of smaller arm muscles, which have the potential to fatigue extremely quickly.

20) *Decrease Armpit Angle (Shoulder Adduction):* As the stroke nears the end of the pull or power phase, and transitions to the exit, the stroke-side arm should come closer to the body. This should also help to facilitate keeping the blade close to the side of the boat. This is yet another example as to the manner in which many of these technical concepts are interrelated.

21) *Imagine a Hula-Hoop:* This concept, when executed properly, is very similar, yet still different from *power circle #2*. The paddler should try to imagine that there is a hula-hoop just below his/her arms, and that he/she must bend it in a downwards motion towards the boat or water. That which provides assistance to the paddler's visualization is to inform him/her that the hula-hoop is covered and connected to his/her arms with saran wrap. The athlete must then reflect upon whether he/she should attempt to keep the saran wrap tight, or allow it to stretch and loosen! If the athlete does not compress down with the arms, the saran wrap will be wrinkled and loose, and the powerful connection will be partially lost. This concept is sometimes referred to as the *Two Arms Leverage System*, whereby the athlete tries to *clamp down* with the top arm, while the sensation exists that the arms are moving closer together.

22) *Imagine an Egg Shell:* In terms of maintaining a tight and compact structure, this is a balancing act that can be thought of in the following manner. Imagine that there is a huge egg that is being held up between the arms. If too little pressure is applied, the egg will drop, and fall into the lap of the paddler. It is better to crush or crack the egg slightly than to let it fall and crash in its entirety. Remember to keep that egg up and balanced between the arms.

23) *Visualize an Umbrella:* This concept can be thought of as a postural picture with regards to the dispersal of one's efforts or *generation of force*. As a simple, yet powerful, exercise, the paddler should be instructed to imagine holding an open umbrella above his or her head. It becomes immediately obvious that the metal support structures branch off from the *centre* in a multitude of directions, and then angle back down towards the "holder" of the umbrella. In a sense, these metal support structures can be imaged as power lines, which change slightly and get modified throughout the stroke. When taking a stroke, similar to **hula-hoop # 21 (saran wrap)**, the kayaker should try to create a firm compression downward with the arms and shoulders, while at the same time, he/she should attempt to bend the shaft of the paddle inward towards the body, thus creating an *umbrella* throughout the stroke. Furthermore, this concept also embodies some **tensegrity** characteristics, due to the opposing forces of compression and tension. The compression has been explained above; however, the tension exists in trying to sit up in a very vertical position, and in lengthening out the vertebrae as much as possible. This posture requires the paddler to perform the ultimate oxymoron: to be rigid and powerful, yet flexible, all at the same time!

24) *Visualize the Movement of a Cat:* A cat has a gait that appears almost effortless; it appears to tread very lightly without disturbing its surroundings. This mental picture can be applied to kayaking as well. The very important question to be posed at this juncture is, "How does one achieve all of the transitions between the four phases of the kayak stroke in as effortless and seamless a manner as is possible?" Minimizing the *airtime* and *pause* between strokes is definitely part of the answer.

25) *Create A Whip Like Effect:* Perhaps this metaphor can assist in solidifying the visualization of the *cat-like motion* (in terms of the exit and recovery/air work phases of the stroke.) For another visual exercise, the paddler should imagine cracking a whip. When an individual knows how to do this well, it is amazing to see how fast, powerful and accurate this motion can be! In the kayak, this motion can be transferred to help execute an extremely swift *recovery* so that virtually no time is wasted before setting up for the successive *catch*. This movement is very similar to the hip flick, or the hip and torso motion of a Brazilian Samba dancer.

26) *Image a Tornado (or Funnel):* As most are aware, a tornado has a very wide diameter at the top, but a very narrow diameter at the bottom. In a kayak, the body should move in this manner as well. Although the hips can only rotate up to a certain point, the s h o u l - ders can rotate and swing to a much greater extent. While this is not so much a technical concept, it does help to give yet another analogy that may be useful for the paddler. He/she should visualize how gross movements up top can and must assist in   contributing   to fine, precise, yet powerful movements down low. When paddling a kayak, the bottom of the *tornado* splits off in two directions, towards the constant contact points in the boat; these being (as spoken about previously) the buttocks and the feet/heels.

27) *Create the Sensation of Water Moving Past Very Fast:* This is not so much a structural or technical concept; rather, it is an assessment or speed check, in relation to the effort that is being exerted when working on particular concepts. At times, human nature being what it is, the possibility exists that one can get overly focused on a particular or specific concept; so much so, that it can actually inhibit boat run. Although this is not normally the case, it is a good idea, every once in a while, to back off mentally just a bit in order to sense and feel the speed of the water moving past the boat. In other words, the kayaker should not forget to maximize boat speed for a specific intensity by feeling the sensation of the higher speed. *Water Moving Past Very Fast* can and should be utilized on a regular basis. (This concept has particular similarities that resemble **Lock the Blade and Glide**.)

I feel that at this juncture, it should be noted that when learning any new technical or structural concept, the athlete should attempt, in the initial stages, to overemphasize the principal idea. Obviously in a race situation, the mental concentration on **Power Circles**, or **Complementary Structural and Technical Concepts** will be quite minimal, if not completely absent. Nevertheless, one can assume that these are all deeply embedded within the paddler's psyche. It is for this reason, that especially during an intense practice, the paddler must take full advantage of this opportunity to solidify these concepts as autonomous components of his/her general kayaking structure. Ultimately, all factors being equal, it is important for the paddler to realize that one should never *paddle pretty* just for the sake of looking pretty; rather, whatever modifications the athlete makes to his/her structure or technique should eventually translate into a faster and more efficient boat speed (despite potential temporary setbacks.)

Chapter 7
Skills and Drills

This ***Skills & Drills*** chapter focuses on various significant practical concepts that are not necessarily directly related, but rather indirectly related, in terms of creating a holistic technical and structural kayaking framework. The **skills and drills** that I outline below will serve well to further supplement and build upon previous ideas. Some drills may not be necessary for some paddlers; however, based on the needs of a particular athlete, the coach can and should make an informed decision as to which drill(s) should take precedence.

Over the many years I have trained in this sport with Dr. Imre Kemecsey, he has devised two simple, but extremely effective, pedagogical methods for teaching paddlers to harmoniously combine different technical concepts. The **Blender** and **Scales Programs** work in the following manner. As an example, the **blender program** can be used to combine two different **power circles** together (e.g. **power circle** #1, two strokes; **power circle** #2, two strokes; and then back to **power circle** #1 ... and so forth.) Once the paddler can perform the **blender program** proficiently, he/she can then embark on the **scales program**. This is a limitless plan of varying permutations and combinations whereby one goes up the *scales* and possibly back down again; much as a musician would when practicing (e.g. two strokes #1; two strokes #3; two strokes #5; two strokes #3; two strokes #1.) Each component of the **blender** and **scales programs** should be done for at least two strokes (left and right sides), prior to proceeding to the next concept. This is necessary in the attempt to avoid any potential miniscule bilateral deficit (a muscular imbalance.) Both the **blender program** and **scales program** encompass not only physical exercise, but also mental exercise. They are also of enormous use in bridging the gap between various **power circles** and **complementary structural and technical concepts**.

Having conversed with several paddlers who have decided to supplement their training with these methods, we have debated as to the best distance for working on various combinations. It has been determined (with ample room for individual flexibility), that any less that 500 meters is too short, as this distance will not allow one the time needed to get into a "good" rhythm. Over 1000 meters, there is the risk that boredom may set in; also, it may prove difficult to maintain concentration due to mental and physical fatigue. It is, therefore, highly important to vary the focus while keeping these principles in mind.

1) *Figure Eights (8s) and Circles:* Following a sufficient warm-up, *figure eights and circles* are an effective way to further enhance and complement the warm-up process. A *figure eight* is exactly as it sounds. The paddler should paddle his/her boat in the pattern of a number "8". A *circle* is achieved by paddling continuously in the shape of a circle (be sure to practice this going in both directions.) There are a few key components that should be adhered to when paddling *figure eights* and *circles* (Figures 7.1 and 7.2):

a) When turning to the left, push the *tiller* (steering stick) all the way to the left; when paddling to the right, push the *tiller* all the way to the right.

b) Lean the boat in the opposite direction to the turn. When turning to the left, lean to the right; when turning to the right, lean to the left.

c) Attempt to lean the boat as much as is possible without getting water into it.

d) Sit in an upright position, and paddle technically and structurally well throughout the turns.

e)The inside foot may need to be pulled out from under the footstrap; this will depend upon the type of boat one is paddling. Both feet can then be placed beside each other back under the footstrap, with the *tiller* pushed to the inside of the turn. Once the turn has been completed, the same technique should be employed on the opposite side, and so forth in succession on alternating sides (***figure eights.***)

f)Follow the same path over and over again in the water, and make the turns as tight as is technically possible, while still taking ``normal`` forward strokes. The paddler should be aware that he/she must allow plenty of room for turning errors.

g)Paddle at varying speeds, and sense the diverse reactions of the boat. Nevertheless, always maintain control of the boat; never allow it to "have a mind of its own!"

I recall that when I first commenced practising this exercise, my choice was to work mainly on ***figure eights*** as opposed to ***circles***. However, my preference has changed over time; I now prefer to practice the ***circles*** for a variety of reasons. The ***circles*** flow in a more continuous pattern, and will allow for far less interruption in the rhythm of the turn. Furthermore, this is a very fine drill for long distance paddlers. This will aid greatly in the development of comfort and stability in the wash or waves; it will also assist the paddler in achieving faster turns, with less need to slow down. I have yet to find a skill or drill that is better in terms of developing a high degree of stability or comfort for all paddlers, regardless of level ... from beginners to the very elite, and everyone in between. **If you have "stability issues", practice this drill over and over again!!!** I cannot over-emphasize this. This drill will further enhance the neuromuscular connection; this includes kinaesthetic awareness as well as proprioceptive neuromuscular facilitation.

There are, indeed, "different strokes for different folks"! Prior to the commencement of many of my important races, while other paddlers would be warming up with ***starts***, I would be practising ***mainly figure eights***, with a few ***starts*** added in for good measure. I recall being on the receptive end of some strange looks ... and comments too! However, this worked very well for me; this drill routine assisted me in "getting into my own world", and I believe, gave me the best possible chance of achieving *flow*. Also, my pre-race anxiety was greatly reduced; these exercises proved to provide both physical and mental assistance. Furthermore, I also felt much more comfortable, physically, before a race, due to the fact that *figure eights* and *circles* enabled me with the potential of being able to loosen up my legs, hips and lower back in a most effective manner. Additionally, once the race or practice began, I also found I was able to perform the *sideways c* and *lean to the stroke-side* far more effectively, confidently, and most importantly, autonomously.

This drill can also be practiced in K-2 and K-4, but one must be cautious at first, as this routine can be much more difficult to do confidently and correctly in a team boat. With practice, however, it should not be a problem.

Figure Eight Pattern: Circles Patterns: (clockwise and counter clockwise)

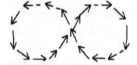

Figure 7.1   Figure 7.2

2) *Ten Strokes, Lean Left; Ten Strokes, Lean Right*: For this drill, the athlete should take ten strokes while leaning the boat to the left, and ten strokes while leaning the boat to the right. Although this may appear very awkward, it is a good drill in terms of developing confidence as to just how far one should, and could, lean the boat. Furthermore, this drill will also encourage and, ultimately, force the kayaker into taking an increasingly active role in terms of controlling the rocking motion of the boat. Yet again, I emphasize that one must take control of the kayak, and not vice versa.

3) *Lean The WRONG Way!* I have found this drill to be one of the most effective methods for solidifying *leaning the boat to the*

stroke-side (which is the correct modality.) As mentioned previously, most uninformed or beginner kayakers, regardless of any previous discipline, have a natural tendency to lean the boat away from the stroke-side. Unfortunately, this practice will most definitely contribute to a substandard connection. Once the paddler is proficient at leaning toward the stroke-side, he/she should be advised to purposely lean away from the stroke-side. The first time I did this, I was amazed at how awkward and incorrect this felt. In leaning the boat away from the stroke-side, I found it to be extremely difficult to engage my legs and rotate properly. I wondered how anyone could possibly paddle in this manner! I am thoroughly convinced that within a very short span of time, all kayakers will report that this position feels very awkward, indeed. After completing this drill, and reverting back to the correct way of leaning the boat to the pulling-side, it will feel just that much more comfortable, solid, and correct.

4) *Feel the Waterwall:* A useful drill for feeling the effect of the *waterwall* is to paddle normally at high speed, and then to move the *tiller/rudder* quickly to one side. This is done in order to magnify the manner in which the boat responds when being compressed into the *waterwall.* One can try this drill by ceasing to paddle as soon as the turn is made; or, one can continue to paddle while turning (remembering to alternate sides).

5) *Slalom*: In similar fashion to a whitewater paddler or a skier, the object of this drill is for the flatwater paddler to zigzag through gates or buoys, so that he/she will experience the effect and support of the *waterwall* against the side of the boat. This drill might be thought of as the midpoint between *twisting/edging the boat.* (Chapter 6, # 5 & 8 and *figure eights/circles*)

6) *Starts*: Performing a *start* in practice is probably the most difficult skill or drill to execute correctly. As stated previously, *starts* are the exercises used most commonly by paddlers prior to the commencement of a race. In training, *starts* should always be practiced on both sides, irrespective of one's preferred side. This is important in terms of minimizing the potential for a neuromuscular imbalance, or bilateral deficit (uneven development.) Furthermore, as a kayaker, one never knows when he/she may need to start on the non-preferred side due to paddling with various K-2 or K-4 partners. In terms of the

structure and technique behind the actual *start*, following is a brief overview of my thoughts:

a)Relax with paddle resting on legs/knees until one hears the instructions "Attention Please", "Start within 10 Seconds", or "Ready - Set". At such time, bring the paddle up to the *ready position.*

b)Prior to taking the first stroke, the stroke-side leg/knee should be in partial extension, in preparation to press vigorously against the footboard, and the torso should be partially rotated forward.

c)*Ready Position*: The blade should be breaking the water surface just slightly; the blade should not be fully planted in the water as this position will provide too much resistance for the first stroke. Of course, the blade should not be totally out of the water either, as this will lead to too much velocity; this, in turn, will limit the force that can be applied to the first stroke (*force/ velocity relationship*).

d)The best angle for the blade should occur naturally. One need not focus on this aspect unless an extraordinary situation presents itself.

e)The top hand should be next to the ear.

f)The first stroke should not be a full stroke. Approximately two-thirds of the length will probably be much more effective; the stroke should subsequently be lengthened out in a gradual manner.

g)Neither arm (elbow) should be in a totally straight, extended position.

h)The torso should be in slight hip flexion (bent forward), and upon taking the first few strokes, the torso can alternate between hip extension and flexion in order to assist with developing momentum in the *sagital* plane. Once the boat is up to speed, however, this torso extension and flexion should cease.

i)When racing in a K-1, there is no one general or particular response as to the number of "long powerful strokes" and "short quick strokes" one should take, prior to getting into *race pace.* Having a really clean start is one of the most difficult feats to accomplish in paddling; if it does not go as well as planned, one should be willing and able to adapt.

j)The ultimate objective is to get into *race pace* as quickly as possible. With abundant practise, each paddler will eventually discover that which works most effectively for him/her. In team boats, obvious accommodations must be made with regards to an initial starting plan, so as to allow for all paddlers to be "on the same page". My unwavering advice at this point is that the more one practises *starts*, the less chance there is that there will be any unwelcome surprises on race day.

7)*Timed Start Drill*: The objective of this routine is to see how quickly one can get his/her boat up to speed over a very limited distance, equal to the length of the kayak (K-1 = 5.2 meters; K-2 = 6.5 meters; K-4 = 11 meters.) The paddler should position the bow of the kayak next to a buoy or a fixed object in the water; the objective is to determine the amount of time needed to get the stern of the kayak to the same fixed point. Obviously, a coach or a fellow athlete will need to time this drill with a stopwatch.

8)*Paddle Backwards and Start*: The idea behind this drill is to increase the degree of difficulty and resistance required in order to get the boat moving forward. To execute this drill, the paddler should take a number of strokes backwards, and then when satisfied, he or she should try a *start*. The ultimate goal is to see how quickly one can get the boat moving forward at *race pace*.

9)*Shoot The Boat*: I also refer to this drill as the *Real Finish*. The best time to practise *shooting* is when the paddler is close to exhaustion. At the conclusion of a very close race, particularly in a 200, one will often see athletes *shooting* their boats. This is done on an individual basis by each paddler in an attempt to increase the probability that he/she will win, or beat out, a particular opponent. Races are frequently won (or lost!) by thousandths of a second; therefore, this is definitely a drill worth practising. In order to *shoot the boat* correctly, timing is everything! Consequently, it is crucial to be comfortable *shooting* off from both the left and right sides. All too often a kayaker may be very comfortable *shooting* his/her boat from only one side, and this should be rectified as soon as possible. It is crucial that the athlete learns to *shoot* his/her boat before the finish line. Once the finish line has been crossed, it is a wasted endeavour! On the flip side, if one *shoots* the boat too early, one will ultimately lose forward momentum at a crucial point, and a very important stroke will have been lost. As stated previously, the best time to practise *shooting the boat* is when one is tired, as this will mimic one's exhaustion level at the conclusion of a hard race. Taking into account that no paddler feels totally fresh at the end of a race, I believe that athletes should be encouraged by their coaches to practise *shooting* their boats at the end of **most distance pieces** in training. This should apply whether one is paddling alone or in a group; this should be done with the recognition that, obviously, a faster boat will produce a quicker time, regardless of any other external factors. In an attempt to comprehend just how and why one would choose to *shoot the boat* at the finish line, the kayaker should throw his/her torso vigorously backwards, so that the boat will accelerate forward with greater speed than it would, simply by taking a normal stroke. This is best explained by Newton's Third Law of Motion, which states that for every action, there is an equal and opposite reaction. A number of the world's top 200 meter sprinters are so powerful and effective at *shooting* their boats, that they are able to get almost their entire bows out of the water!

10)*Shoot Drill*: While the kayaker is paddling, he/she should practice *shooting* the boat off of every stroke. This may seem very strange at first, but eventually this exercise will strengthen the various muscles (hip extensors, etc.) that are needed for *shooting* the boat. Furthermore, by practicing this drill on every stroke, it will minimize the potential for favouring one side or developing a bilateral deficit. As well, the paddler will gain ease, comfort, and agility in *shooting the boat*. It should be noted that this drill can be modified, if necessary, to allow for greater boat speed, so that the *shoot* seems more realistic and/or applicable. For example, a paddler might attempt to *shoot* on every 3rd, 5th, or 7th stroke. It is, however, important that the athlete always *shoots* the boat on an odd number stroke, so that the drill will switch sides from left to right, and vice versa.

11)*Remove The Footboard*: This drill has been mentioned previously in Chapter 3. Nevertheless, as a reminder, by removing the footboard, the athlete's nervous system will be forced to find alternate methods of transferring momentum or energy into the boat that do not ultimately transform into a seesawing (pitch) action. Furthermore, paddlers, at the request of their coaches, might do a little experimentation by pressing down into the bottom of the boat or footboard with the heels of their feet. I have found that this, too, can be effective at minimizing *bouncing* motions.

12)*Remove The Rudder*: This is not only a beneficial drill for learning to equalize the *torques* (*snaking*), but this drill will also indicate whether there is a major left or right bilateral preference. Every paddler has imbalances, some more than others, and this is to be considered as a natural manifestation of the human body. However, by removing the rudder only once in a while, this will amplify the impact that the athlete is having on the boat, and he/she will develop a greater sense and state of equilibrium. To quote Imre Kemecsey, "A kayak is not an aircraft carrier." Every move one takes or makes will either have a positive or negative effect on *boat run*. Remember to carefully tape up the opening, on the hull of the kayak, after removing the rudder.

13)*Potato Knapsack Drill*: ***Take Extreme Caution with this Drill*** During this exercise, the athlete wears a knapsack, and fills it with very light weights (5-10 lbs.), or a number of potatoes. The knapsack should, ideally, be snug up against the back, but loose enough on the straps so that the paddler can remove it in an emergency, such as in the unlikely event that he/she should fall into the water. (I would prefer no drowning, please, and certainly not with the additional added weight!) This drill is meant to help exaggerate the *rotation* in combination with the *full swing* and the *whip*. See (Chapter 6, #16 and #25) This will also assist in teaching *sooner body rotation* (Chapter 2, #2), which is a crucial element to the initiation of the entire stroke. Prior to doing this drill on the water, the paddler should be encouraged to practise both seated and standing variations, while emphasizing flicking the hip forward, following later with the torso, and ultimately involving the shoulders.

14)*Resistor Workout (Headwind Simulation)*: Although many are familiar with this drill, I will reiterate the beneficial components, as well as the manner in which it should be practised. Using a resistor is an excellent way to allow for *slow motion*; this, in turn, will enhance sensation and observation in terms of improving structure as well as general components of technique. The oxymoron is to attempt to make the boat glide as consistently as is possible, while at the same time, limiting the boat's ability to glide. If the kayaker can learn to paddle economically with a resistor, then paddling without one will feel that much easier. I have found that using a resistor can help a great deal in terms of learning to maintain the *bent shaft* (Chapter 2, #1), and/or the *ice-cream effect*. (Chapter 6, #18) This can also be referred to as *spreading the stroke*, whereby it should be emphasized that a powerful *exit* or *support before recovery* (Chapter 2, #5) is just as important, if not more so, than a powerful *catch*. This is particularly true in K-1. When practicing this drill, *air-time* or *recovery* should also be kept to an absolute minimum so as to minimize loss of momentum. It should also be noted that resistors can be very useful devices for coaches in terms of keeping paddlers of different speeds together during a workout. Obviously, the faster paddler should use a larger resistor. Resistors are also a significant tool for paddlers who have stroke rates that are too high (avoid the *Fred Flintstone effect* – Chapter 6, #18); in addition, they are able to provide assistance to athletes who may have dynamic stability issues. Resistors may take many forms, shapes, styles, and sizes; almost anything can be used that one is able to tie to, or around, a boat! I have witnessed the use of bungee cords, ropes, ropes with tennis balls on them, and even buckets. Resistors can be tied around the bow or the stern of the kayak; however, I would recommend the stern in an attempt to avoid splashing oneself!

15)*Bungee Cord Workout*: In preparation for this exercise, one end of a rope/bungee cord needs to be anchored to a fixed point on a dock or on the shore, and the other end needs to be tied around the cockpit of the kayak. The athlete will start to paddle slowly, gradually building tension on the bungee cord until he/she cannot move any further forward. At this point the paddler needs to try to maintain his/her position in the water, while practicing the directives of the coach. This drill is very similar to the *resistor workout* discussed above; *stroke length* will need to be maximized, and *air-time* will need to be minimized. Once the athlete has completed the *set* or *piece*, he/she should keep paddling and decrease effort gradually, in order to ensure that the boat does not slam back into the dock. This is a remarkable way to work on *interval training*, especially in an environment with limited space. *Bungee cord workouts* can even be practiced in pools, assuming this will be allowed in any given pool **and assuming that there is water in the pool!**

16)*Support Drill*: This is an extremely beneficial exercise, due to the fact that after a relatively very short period of time has elapsed, the athlete will be able to feel a major contrast between an interconnected body, as opposed to a body not working as an interconnected unit. In Part A of the drill, the coach should call out various *support components*, and the paddler will gradually build up (from the bottom up) the entire internal structure, in a step-by-step format. In Part B of the drill, the coach should instruct the athlete to gradually eliminate various levels of support. This, of course, will degrade the entire structure, with the resultant effect and intent that the kayaker will again be able to feel a major contrast between a superior and a substandard connection.

Part A
1. the water is supporting the front of the boat
2. the footrest is supporting the legwork
3. the legs are supporting the gluteus muscles
4. the gluteus muscles are supporting the rotation of the hips
5. the hips are supporting the rotation of the lower part of the trunk
6. the lower part of the trunk is rotating 4-7 centimetres
7. the upper part of the trunk is rotating 20-40 centimetres
8. the upper part of the trunk is supporting the shoulders (deltoid muscles)
9. the shoulders are supporting the arms
Part B
1. the water is not supporting the front of the boat
2. the footrest is not supporting the legwork
3. the legs are not supporting the gluteus muscles
4. the gluteus muscles are not supporting the rotation of hips
5. the hips are not supporting the rotation of the lower part of the trunk

6. the rotation of the lower part of the trunk is not supporting the rotation of the upper part of the trunk (shoulders)

7. the shoulders (deltoid muscles) are not supporting the arms

By temporarily limiting the relationship or union between interdependent body components, the intention is that in the athlete will gradually develop a keener awareness and greater ability for *self* error detection, cause, and correction.

17)*Earlier Body Rotation (Mirror):* This is one of the few drills that I shall discuss which cannot be practiced in the kayak; rather, it should be practiced in the gym or at home. The only equipment required is a large mirror. At first, and while standing, focus on the *sooner body rotation*, at the same time initiating it with an earlier stroke-side leg in conjunction with the hips; exaggerate the motion. Try, also, to focus on the fact that the hips can only move a predetermined amount, whereas the upper torso will follow, and ultimately *unwind* in a smooth, precise and controlled manner. Finally, imagine that the hands are the blades of the paddle, and finish with the hand moving backwards, just before the rotation to the opposite side commences. This drill may seem simple, and it does not require a lot of physical effort; nevertheless, it is significant with respect to mental training. Over time, one should experience considerable improvement in regards to the sequencing of these movements. Once the athlete is able to perform this drill correctly, he/she should then try this exercise in a seated position, with the feet placed against an immovable object, in an attempt to imitate the sensation of the feet on the footboard.

18)*Kayak Ergometer:* Over the past few years, the kayak ergometer has evolved substantially, and many top kayakers now utilize them to augment training regimens. It is for this reason, that I shall briefly discuss some of the benefits, as well as some of the limitations, of the ergometer. Although there are quite a few models on the market today, one of the most popular, and one that I have used in particular, is the SpeedStroke by KayakPro. This machine is highly impressive with regards to all the features with which it comes equipped on the on-board console. Some of these distinctive aspects include, but are not limited to, data regarding distance, time, stroke rate, heart rate, power output, elapsed time, speed, and projected speed. Obviously, as a coach and/or athlete, having access to this data can be extremely valuable. Nevertheless, that which I hold in even higher priority is having the ability to practice one's stroke in a controlled environment, without having the opportunity to *hide* in the boat. When working on the ergometer, almost everything, both good and not so good, is visible. Furthermore, when living in colder climates, or when the weather is not conducive to paddling on the water, the ergometer, although not perfect, provides an excellent option for a diligent workout. In terms of ergometer limitations, it is important to realize that although it is a significant piece of exercise equipment, it is **not** a kayak. Clearly, stability issues are not much of an issue when working on the ergometer, and one might gain a false sense of mastery of the sport of kayaking if the ergometer is used to excess, or instead of actual kayaking. Finally, a major difference that others have experienced, myself included, between actual paddling and using the ergometer, is that there is much more of an emphasis on the *catch* with the ergometer, and it is far more difficult to truly *spread the stroke*. With regards to the *exit* and the *recovery/air-work*, it feels as if the imaginary *blade* wants to pop out of the imaginary water. Also, the sensation does not embody the same degree of *smoothness* as when paddling on the water; this is due to the lack of cable tension at the end of the stroke. As already mentioned, this machine seems to force the athlete to load up the *catch* to a much greater extent, perhaps because it may be too difficult to *spread the stroke* or find that final support before the *recovery* (probably more applicable for Team Boats, K-2 and K-4.) In summation, the kayak ergometer is a noteworthy training tool; however, it is important to be aware of its potential drawbacks as well.

Chapter 8
Paddling Team Boats (K-2 & K-4)

The sport of kayaking is one of a limited number that can be considered both an individual and a team sport. On a personal level, the aspects of flexibility, opportunity for variation, as well as parallel skill development, have always created a tremendous amount of excitement and gratification for me.

In general, paddling team boats is more similar than dissimilar as compared to paddling singles or K-1s. Nevertheless, there are certain differences upon which I shall digress at this juncture. It should be noted that paddling a team boat requires, of the paddler, a very different skill set. Furthermore, one should not assume or take for granted that technical and structural ideas that are desirable or appropriate for singles and K-1s are always appropriate or applicable with respect to paddling team boats.

Probably the most significant and obvious factor regarding team boats is that one cannot just do as he/she so desires at any given moment; rather, all partners must adapt and compromise with one-another, so as to work together as a cohesive unit. I have witnessed, on numerous occasions, the manner in which team boats, comprised of those who are slower paddlers in singles and K-1's, have been able to win against faster paddlers. Did these winning boats suddenly become faster in a matter of minutes? No, of course not! Did the faster **team** boat work better as a **team**? Perhaps; this observation brings me to the obvious question, "What are the necessary parameters in which this can occur?"

One of the major factors that I have observed with regards to the best team boats is the timing. I am not merely examining the merits of the paddle blades catching and recovering at the same time; rather, I am taking into account the fact that the legs, the hips, the torso, and the shoulders of each individual paddler are all working together in a balanced, cohesive, unison. The best team boat paddlers move as if they are components of a perfectly tuned machine, or a world class orchestra. In fact, one could certainly compare this to an intricate dance. Seeing a good crew working together in perfect unison is definitely an artistic sight for me to behold! Without doubt, the best way to achieve this type of perfection is through good coaching and time spent working together in the boat.

In previous chapters, I have discussed the importance of **spreading the stroke**, and having a **powerful support before recovery** when paddling solo. It should be noted that this does not necessarily apply in team boats; I have observed that many of the best doubles, K-2s and K-4s exert their energies in a different manner. Very often one will see that these paddlers execute three interrelated acts. Firstly, they **load up the catch** (*everything up front*); secondly, they develop a very distinct rhythm; thirdly, they allow more of a pause between strokes (different cadence) so as to allow the boat to *glide* during the **recovery** or **air work** time. This is by no means any indication that the stroke rate will be any slower; rather, quite to the contrary. In team boats, especially the K-4, the boat speed is considerably higher, so it should come as no surprise that the water will move past at a much higher rate of speed. A *fully loaded* K-4 is obviously much heavier than a K-1, and it will, therefore take much more force to get it up to speed; however, once the speed is achieved, it will be far easier to maintain that speed. This is Newton's Second Law of Motion. For added clarity, this principle can be applied to the comparison of a truck versus a car. The time required to accelerate or decelerate is obviously going to be quicker for the car.

All things being equal, paddlers in team boats are able to maintain their momentum with far less effort, due to the fact that the boats are heavier and there is more power available. Consequently, the **support before recovery** is not required in the same way as it is in a single or K-1, due to the fact that it is not as much of a struggle to maintain momentum during the **recovery** or **air time**. Therefore, it is more effective to increase the stroke-rate, and to get to the next **catch** quickly, provided that the power is present (**power** before **rate**).

Many of the best team boat paddlers discuss not only using their eyes to full advantage, but also employing as many other senses as is possible, in the attempt to work as a truly cohesive unit. These elite paddlers do not only see that which is occurring, they hear it and feel it on an instinctive level! These paddlers are so in tune with one- another, that they are able to complement each other almost to perfection, while still counteracting their partners' temporary potential deficits (an ineffective stroke, etc.) If something feels not quite as it should, a good partner will help to correct the issue or problem in a natural and automatic manner, without overcompensating and ruining the rhythm and holistic structure. Furthermore, it should be noted that it is not only the responsibility of 2nd, 3rd and 4th seat paddlers to follow those in front of them; those paddlers in the stroke position or the 1st seat need to feel, hear, and adapt to what is going on in the back of the boat as well.

I have noted with interest, upon watching close-up videos of doubles, K-2s, and K-4s, that one very common error amongst those paddlers who are following other paddlers in front of them, is a tendency to *rush* the stroke ever so slightly; there is only a minimal chance that a paddler will be late with a stroke. One can ascertain this for oneself by viewing various videos, and pressing the pause button mid-stroke. I have seen videos of some of the top world class K-2s and K-4s, wherein the paddlers in the back are rushing. Being aware of this glaring inaccuracy, I feel compelled to ask two questions.

1. Why are some of these paddlers, particularly at this high level of expertise, not working in complete synchrony?
2. What is the best way to go about correcting these errors?

Firstly, as a paddler who has spent my fair share of time in the back of team boats, I would say that many athletes may worry slightly, perhaps on a subconscious level, about keeping up with those in front of him/her. Unfortunately, this concern or restlessness (especially in a race) may cause overcompensation if one is not careful; the paddler may devote excess or residual energies to increasing the stroke rate rather than increasing the power. Furthermore, it is also certainly conceivable that the athletes in a particular team boat are working with different stroke lengths; this, as well, can cause a disparity in timing. A lack of having spent enough time practising together in a particular boat may contribute to timing issues; this is particularly true if the paddler in the stroke or 1st seat position changes the stroke rate rhythm abruptly and frequently, without any or adequate warning. Finally, muscular fatigue is also a factor that should not be overlooked.

In the final section of this chapter, I outline four specific drills that are particularly useful when paddling team boats. These exercises have been proven time and again in assisting with increasing the level of cohesiveness in any particular team boat.

1.*Hit Early, Hit Late & Hit On Time Drill*: This drill is one that encourages the paddler(s) in the back of a team boat to practice timing; this is accomplished by being early at first, then late, and subsequently, exactly in unison. The theory is that if one has had experience in comprehending the feel, look, and sound when the timing is out of synch, then it will be less likely that this will occur in a race situation. Furthermore, if the stroke-timing happens to break down, the athlete should be able to self correct his/her errors much more easily and promptly.

2.*Blindfold Drill*: In this drill, all paddlers in the kayak who are not sitting in the 1st seat, and are, therefore, not responsible for steering, wear a blindfold. The concept behind this drill is to eliminate one sense in order to heighten the other senses. At first this drill will seem rather alien, and one will quickly realize the extent to which one depends on one's eyes for guidance. Nevertheless, with practise the other senses will develop a greater ability to compensate. This drill is excellent for developing kinaesthetic awareness and proprioceptive abilities.

3.*Pause Drill*: The following two drills are not necessarily team boat drills. Nevertheless, I have found them to be of particular benefit for developing an increased sense of comfort and cohesiveness in team boats. After a predetermined set of strokes, the athlete(s) is/ are required to *pause* mid-stroke during the ***recovery*** or ***air-work*** for approximately 1-2 seconds, while allowing the kayak to glide. Different variations of this exercise should be practised regarding the amount of strokes leading up to the *pause*. I suggest starting with 7 strokes, 5 strokes, 3 strokes and then every stroke. The paddler will notice that this drill should always be practiced with an odd number of strokes, so that it will alternate between left and right sides.

4.*Power Drill*: The **power drill** should be practiced in a very similar manner to the **pause drill**, but rather than pausing, the athlete(s) should *power up* the boat as much as is possible, with only one stroke. Again, the power strokes should be done on an odd number so that the exercise will alternate from side to side; 7 strokes, 5 strokes, 3 strokes, and then every stroke. It is also important that all paddlers be reminded that there should be a distinct difference between the *on* and *off* strokes. All too often, and especially when the paddler is tiring, the *on* and *off* strokes blend together. When taking *off* strokes, keep the intensity very low; during the *on* strokes, exert a maximum amount of power.

Chapter 9
Pedagogical, Psychological, and Tactical Considerations

Thus far, the focus of this book has been to convey knowledge regarding execution of a unique and novel approach to kayak structure and technique. Nevertheless, prior to conclusion, I will delve into a few tried and true concepts; these can assist greatly in imparting knowledge to the athlete. Over the years, I have become acutely aware that, regardless of natural ability, an athlete's motivations to improve and adhere to a comprehensive training regimen are additional factors that can contribute to success. As a coach, it is one's task to channel enthusiasm in the appropriate direction, and to get the athlete(s) back *on track* when and if occasional *hiccups* should occur. Of course, it must always be kept in mind that athletes are multifaceted people, *NOT* machines or robots (although some may appear to be!)

There are three basic types of coaching styles: autocratic/dictator; democratic/teacher; and submissive/babysitter. Without any doubt, Imre Kemecsey falls into the democratic/teacher category. As an extremely versatile and progressive coach, it is obvious that his background as a sports psychologist has played a key role in shaping his coaching philosophy, as well as his standard of practice. Rather than pointing out the negative or the incorrect, he finds alternative and positive means to correct technical and structural errors. Negative instructions such as, "Don't bring your arms so low", will only serve to ingrain in the brain precisely that which one is trying to avoid. It is far better to instil within the athlete, positive instructions/affirmations; this is best achieved by making a comment such as, "Keep your arms up". Better yet, direct the athlete to focus on *power circle #2*, or the *saran wrap*, or the *hula-hoop*. By avoiding negative feedback, the likelihood of psychological mastery is increased. Subsequently and consequently, the potential for negative self-talk, negative affirmations, and fear of failure are decreased. These concepts, which I have discussed in depth throughout this book, are causal in my coming to the conclusion that coaching should be conducted by embracing a *holistic approach*. It is not enough to correct an error through critical analysis; rather, one must determine the various causes of errors, and explore the source of deficiencies. Furthermore, when correcting these errors, one must be mindful so as not to create another unintended error or negative consequence.

As stated above, Imre's coaching style is extremely democratic; this is vividly obvious when an athlete comes to him for critical analysis and feedback, upon the completion of a particular exercise. More often than not, Imre will pose a question such as, "How did that feel to you?", rather than immediately impart information regarding technical and structural errors, or criticisms. Imre's method of choice is always geared toward instilling confidence and positive self-talk; he will, therefore, engage the paddler in a brief athlete-centered discussion when appropriate and/or necessary. By doing so, he validates the kayaker's concerns or questions, thereby allowing the athlete to take some responsibility and ownership for his/her goals. As an athlete, I have been trained by a variety of coaches, who have used a variety of pedagogical methods. By comparison, I cannot speak highly enough about Imre's *positive approach*. Imre rarely tells a paddler that he/she is doing anything *wrong* (although, at the given instance, the endeavour may not be entirely correct.) Imre never criticises any of his athletes, and he never requests that he/she correct anything that is not fully understood, thereby minimizing frustration. Alternatively, Imre encourages the athlete to create a kinaesthetic and visual image, and subsequently, urges the paddler to reproduce and refine this image.

From a coach's perspective, it is quite conceivable that one may, upon occasion, do too much of the thinking for an athlete, thereby creating a sense of dependency rather than empowerment. While a loyal and supportive coach is an invaluable resource for the athlete, I do believe that there are instances wherein *less is more*.

From an athlete's perspective, I have personally experienced situations wherein *less is more.* Having previously stated that one should practice technical and structural concepts at high speed in the attempt to ingrain them within the psyche, I do feel that it is also important to know when to back off just a little in terms of intensity; the exception makes the rule! I have found that under certain conditions, an intensity approximating 95% may yield faster times and/or speeds than a 100% all out effort! Perhaps this is due to the fact that at a slightly lower level of exertion, the athlete may be able to compensate technically to a greater extent, and to offset the lower physiological output. Furthermore, while periodization and physiological training factors are outside the scope of this book, it is important to mention that one should not necessarily assume that the fastest athlete is always the one to possess the greatest capacity to perform the most work, in terms of intensity, duration, and volume.

It is also of considerable interest to contemplate the difference between perceived maximal physical exertion and absolute maximal physical exertion. It is almost inconceivable for an athlete to perform to the top of his/her physiological capabilities, when training in isolation, or without training partners. Both in training and racing situations, it is obvious that the athlete who will derive the greatest physiological benefit is the one who competes consistently against other paddlers who are at a similar level in terms of ability and/or speed. If one is much faster than his/her competition, he/she cannot be pushed. The same effect will occur if one is much slower than the competition. However, the proven oxymoron in these situations is that when competing with and against athletes with similar abilities, these training sessions and/or races will usually be the most beneficial and demanding because the outcome and expectations are *uncertain.*

One **mind game** in particular, that I have observed, I will now briefly touch upon; this concerns itself with regards to athlete interaction. On numerous occasions, prior to a training session or a race, an athlete may complain to another that he/she is tired, and not feeling up to par; however, once on the water, the paddler in question performs very well. True enough, there may be days in which the paddler does not feel as adequate as on other days; however, if this happens too often, whether the athlete recognizes it or not, he/she is setting up a defence mechanism as an excuse for the potential of an inferior performance. A paddler such as this may have a fear of failure. In such instances, the coach should discourage this kind of public comment or negative self talk. When and if possible, it is important to avoid all negative self-fulfilling prophesies.

Another scenario that I have witnessed with regret, time and time again during training sessions, can best be described as *picking pieces*. On numerous occasions, I have seen an athlete deliberately hold back during a particular piece in an attempt to recover, so that on the successive piece, he/she can work at a much higher intensity, with the intent of winning or beating the competition. Coaches must recognize that allowing this variation to occur is usually not of benefit to the training group as a whole, and it can create many conflicts over time, if left unaddressed. No paddler wants to be *washed out* by an athlete who was lagging far behind in a previous piece. Every athlete should be encouraged to be as consistent as possible for the entire duration of the workout. This should be considered as *fair play*.

In terms of actual *race plans*, a different scenario unfolds, and reveals itself. Much of that which I have written about in the previous paragraph may not necessarily apply in true race conditions. Ultimately, if one wants to perform to the best of his/her ability, it may be beneficial to engage in some *mind games* in the attempt to gain an edge. One may use whatever means are at his/her disposal, as long as these psychological and/or physical manoeuvres adhere to the rules! The type of race plan employed during a race should depend on a number of factors:

1. the distance being raced
2. the type of boat (e.g. K-1, K-2, or K-4)
3. the speed of one's competitors
4. whether it is a heat, semi-final, or final (and the manner in which the progressions work)
5. the number of races in the day, as well as the amount of recovery time between races
6. the water conditions and weather (e.g. headwind, tailwind, crosswind, and/or temperature)

On many occasions, I have overheard comments on Race Day such as, "Just worry about yourself out there"; "Just race your own race"; or, "Forget about everyone else." I could not disagree more! Although an athlete should have a general plan as to the manner in which to approach each race, one also needs to be flexible and adaptable, based on the various factors that have been listed above. Practising a time control in training is obviously significantly different from an actual race. In major races, many of the most elite paddlers are able to enact a contingency plan should things not go as planned. These athletes do not stress out and fall apart; rather, they realize that the race is not over until the finish line is crossed. They have the ultimate confidence in their abilities, regardless of external factors.

There are many types of race plans, each embodying its own set of intricate details, which go into its development. These are employed with great success. Following, is a synopsis of three general types:

1.*All Out*: This type of plan is used by the paddler who works as intensely as possible, and attempts to hold off others for as long as possible. When using this type of plan, the athlete will slow down a great deal towards the end of a race, due to overwhelming fatigue. I do not recommend this type of race plan for any distance other than 200 meter races or less.

2.*Conventional*: This type of race plan is the most common. It involves the typical explosive start, then settling into a race pace wherein one is, hopefully, able to be in contention with the top paddlers in the race, various *pick-ups* throughout the distance, and a solid finish involving increasing intensity.

3.*Come From Behind*: This type of race plan is most commonly used for longer distances, such as 1000 meters or above. In order to execute this kind of plan correctly, the athlete must be overwhelmingly confident in his/her abilities. Basically, the paddler will sit back just a bit during the beginning stages of the race, and subsequently he/she will gradually try to move up on the competition, passing others one at a time. It is important that the athlete maintains contention with the early leaders so that he/she does not fall back to the point where the distance to be made up is far too great. The ability to pace oneself is of great significance in this type of race. This is often no easy feat!

There are two particular types of training exercises that I believe are most beneficial for assisting an athlete in learning to pace himself/herself correctly:

1.Fartlek Training: *Fartlek* is a Swedish term meaning *speed play*. In utilizing this method of training, a paddler will take turns leading the others in a particular training group, without advising the group members as to when he/she intends to accelerate or take the lead. This manner of training encourages each paddler to keep his/her guard up at all times, and to be prepared to accelerate at any given moment. *Fartlek training* usually occurs in a *wash-riding* situation, but it can be employed in other situations as well. *Wash-Riding* occurs when a paddler utilizes another paddler's *bow wave* in order to decrease the energy needed to sustain an equivalent speed. It is very comparable to the manner in which cyclists draft off of each other. This manoeuvre will feel as if the paddler is going *downhill*. The position of the kayak must be slightly behind and to the side of the paddler who is in the lead; one's bow should be positioned beside the other athlete's blade of his/her paddle. Whoever is in the lead at any particular moment will need to expend the most energy, whereas those paddlers on the sides will be using much less energy. Sometimes a paddler may get between and slightly behind two other paddlers; from this vantage point, he/she will be able to ride the *V Wash*. This is the easiest position in which to find oneself, as it will be possible to ride (almost surf!) double the wash. This is referred to as the *V Wash* due to the obvious fact that the wash will come back from the two boats which are ahead in the shape of a *V*. In both training and long distance races, any paddler can take turns with the others to be in the lead position; this will kick up the pace, and make the group more efficient. It is mandatory, however, to position the boat correctly, so that the bow of the boat will submerge slightly. If positioned incorrectly, one may fall off the wash, be washed out, and/or collide with another boat or paddle. This may prove to be a perplexing and troublesome skill to master at the outset, as with the important intent to avoid potential problems, one needs to anticipate the manner in which the boat will react within any given set of circumstances. Repeated practise of this skill is the obvious key to improvement. Nevertheless, it is important not to over-indulge in *wash-riding* during training sessions, as there is the potential for it to cause technical and structural deficits. It is important to note that *wash-riding* is legal only when racing in distances of over 1000 meters.

2.Give-Do-Guess (Pace-Learning Process): This is a type of training process whereby a paddler will *give* a time to the coach prior to the commencement of a piece; one that he/she thinks is attainable and achievable. Then, the athlete will **do** the piece. Finally, the athlete will take a **guess** as to the actual time. The purpose of this process is to train the athlete to be as accurate as is possible regarding the actual times in terms of the **do** and the **guess**. During this mode of training, the athlete should be given the freedom to choose and alternate speeds; obviously this must be within reason.

One final tactical consideration that I will discuss briefly is the adaptations or modifications that should be made when paddling in a variety of conditions. For the most part, the proficient paddler will adjust subconsciously and autonomously to weather, water, and wind changes. Nevertheless, there are a few key concepts that are worth highlighting with regards to this topic. When paddling in a headwind, it is extremely important for one to maximize his/her **stroke-length**; this is achieved by taking long strokes with a powerful support before the **recovery**, so as to minimize the loss of boat speed due to the **air time**. In a tailwind, the **stroke-rate** will naturally increase due to a greater boat speed. This is beneficial and should be encouraged, as long as the power is still evident, and the blades of the paddle are not spinning out of control. Paddling well in a strong, direct crosswind (**toilet paddling**) is the most difficult situation with which to deal; obviously, this type of environmental condition comes with the most challenges. Through training, a paddler must learn to relax as much as possible, and work with the water and wind, rather than against it. It is particularly important to be relaxed, yet still firm in the lower body. Furthermore, when there appears to be a need for greater stability, one can lower the arms slightly; this action will lower the entire center of gravity, thus increasing the stability of the kayak. Nevertheless, I tend to discourage this method whenever possible, as it has the potential to develop or ingrain numerous bad habits over time, if left unchecked.

It is incumbent upon coaches to find ways and means to assist athletes to feel as comfortable and confident as possible. If and when this is accomplished, the athlete will be well on his/her way to achieving self-actualization through *flow*. The concept of *flow* was investigated in great detail by Mihaly Csikszentmihalyi (1975). Csikszentmihalyi said that *flow* is the sensation achieved when an athlete feels himself/ herself to be in a holistic and euphoric state; this is a self-hypnotic sensation, wherein he/she is experiencing total involvement, and is on *automatic pilot!* Csikszentmihalyi also emphasized that *flow* can only be achieved when one's abilities are equivalent to the challenge. Over the years, as both a paddler and a coach, I have become keenly aware and increasingly convinced of the undeniable reality that if a kayaker is able to master many of the holistic concepts which I have previously discussed, these will assist him/her in achieving *flow* far more often than not!

Chapter 10
Final Wrap Up! – "Let it Run!"

At the outset of this book, I mentioned the fact of my having been pleased that I waited a number of years prior to commencing upon the arduous task of putting my thoughts and ideas into writing. Now that I am nearing the conclusion of this creation, I must say that I am absolutely thrilled! The true complexity of coaching kayak technique and structure is an ever changing and dynamic pursuit; I remain convinced that there is still much more to uncover. Speaking on behalf of coaches, I believe it to be crucial that we never remain stagnant; rather, the attempt must always be made to seek out novel and superior ways of imparting knowledge to our fellow colleagues and athletes. It is also essential that we remain confident, yet humble. It is in this manner of *being* that we may embrace, or at least be receptive to, the thoughts, ideas, and comments of others. Over the years, I have become increasingly aware that the more one learns, the more one realizes that there is much more to learn. Although I have attempted to create the most comprehensive and practical manual possible regarding holistic kayak coaching, I am certain that once published, I will be *kicking myself* for having not had the foresight to include new and emerging concepts. Obviously, there will always be room for improvement, and perhaps these concepts will be the beginnings of another piece, reserved for a later time. New instructional metaphors and analogies will continue to emerge, and I challenge the reader to develop some of his/her own. Ultimately, the all-encompassing motive of this pedagogic method is to challenge the ordinary by thinking *outside the box*, and in so doing, altering one's coaching philosophy from a conventional to a holistic approach.

In conclusion, I would like to make crystal clear, that superior kayak technique and structure will never take the place of, or substitute for, a superior physiological foundation. Rather, it will complement and enhance one's ability to the maximum extent. It is also important never to assume that the faster paddler always has better technique (although this may usually be the case.) This is the reason as to the importance of the paddler expending a great deal of time and effort in improving not only his/her strengths, but also in minimizing weaknesses. In the words of Benjamin Franklin, "A small leak can sink a great ship." Pun intended!

As a strong advocate regarding the sport of kayaking, I have taken on numerous roles at different levels and stages over the years. I have the utmost respect and admiration for this sport, and honestly love it in every way possible! In perfect honesty, I cannot imagine anyone not loving the kayak, and every aspect which it entails. In my opinion, as long as one enjoys that in which he/she is involved regarding paddling at least 50% of the time, regardless of role, one should feel it incumbent upon him/herself to do all that is possible in terms of promoting, publicizing, encouraging, and defending the greatest sport on the face of the planet! In summation, I wish my very best to all those involved in this sport, and I embrace to the motto to the Calgary Canoe Club; to me, it signifies an expressive, significant, and meaningful quote with which to close:

"PER AQUAS AD FRATERNITATEM"
"THROUGH THE WATERS TO FRIENDSHIP"

References

Barton, G., & Endicott, W.T. *(1992). The Barton Mold. – A Study in Sprint Kayaking* A publication of the U.S. Canoe and Kayak Team.

British Canoe Union, (2007). *British Canoe Union Coaching Handbook* – British Canoe Union.

Cox, R. W., *(1992). The science of canoeing: A guide for competitors and coaches to understanding and improving performance in sprint and marathon kayaking,* Frodsham, Coxburn.

Ingber, D,E. (January 1998, 48-57) *The Architecture of Life, "Scientific American"*

Kemecsey, I. (1990). *Kemecsey Mental Training.*

Duncan, BC: Priority Printing Ltd.

Martens, R., (1997). *Successful Coaching*

Champaign, IL: Human Kinetics.

Sinclair, D,A. (1995) *Mental Management Resources, B.C. Flatwater Canoe Team.*

Vancouver, BC: Human Performance International.

Weinberg, R,S., & Gould, D., (1995) *Foundations of Sport and Exercise Psychology.*

Champaign, IL: Human Kinetics.

Testimonials

I am lucky enough to be amongst those who can witness and attest to this process, which commenced due to Imre's activity in canoe and kayak technique. Dating from the sixties, this technique has been evolving up until today, and will continue to do so into the future. It spreads from champions and coaches, and is constantly and consistently in a state of development and flux.

Richard Dawkins introduced the Meme Theory, which is the extension of the Theory of Evolution, to a basic cultural unit. The Kemecsey technique is the epitome of one which has become such a basic cultural unit in canoeing and kayaking.

I am always happy to watch the champions of today, who fundamentally paddle with the kayak technique created by Kemecsey. Many are probably not aware of this, and have never met Imre. However, this personal contact is not even necessary; the technique worked out and developed by Imre lives on, spreads, and improves further, thanks to imitation and selection.

Imre could take the position of sitting back and watching this situation with true and well-deserved satisfaction. However, this was never to be! Imre refuses to remain idle, as he is "mad" about canoeing and kayaking. He is unable to function wholly without any theoretic activity. He has, therefore, remained involved, in the successful attempt to continue to produce and advance an educational system; this methodology assists in incorporating the champions' techniques through simplification. Together, he and I worked out the system of *Power Circles* in the canoe technique. Imre then took this technique apart and re-assembled these elements in regards as to the manner in which they interrelate. By practicing the *Power Circles*, one can develop a high level of kayak technique and expertise. How far can one go? Ultimately, it essentially depends on the kayaker's ability. I hope this book will have a significant impact on our sport. On a personal level, I look forward to spreading Imre's *Kayak Meme* further along the kayak waters.

István Vaskuti
6X World Champion, Olympic Champion
International Canoe Federation – Vice President

To understand human movements, to describe them in literary terms, to learn them, and to teach them, is a very complex and complicated task. Coaches and athletes attempt to create varying methods and different theories to assist in increasing the efficiency of the learning process. We can best describe this as a multidisciplinary process which, we intend, will ultimately assist the athlete. I received Imre Kemecsey's book, **The Inner Structure of the Kayak Technique**, many years subsequent to my initiation into the sport of kayaking. This work was revolutionary, unique, and distinct in every way. This book grabbed my attention, and as a computer animator, I decided to create kayak animations for use as a teaching tool in visualizing these theories.

Dari, one of Imre's athletes, steps forward in his book; he summarizes Imre's theories and methodologies in an outstanding way. Indeed, Dari also adds his personal perspectives and points of view. Dari has taken an up-close look at these exercises; additionally, he has further examined the biomechanics, pedagogy, and psychology of paddling, and has shed light on the manner in which these factors interrelate and coexist amongst one another. Dari has demonstrated a superior ability in highlighting pedagogical and psychological elements.

Thank you to Dari Y. Fisher and to Imre Kemecsey for their pioneer works.

Zoltan Varga

This book, written under the guidance and instruction of Dr. Imre Kemecsey, represents an abundance of the most novel, inclusive concepts, regarding the technique of flatwater kayaking. It treats the subject matter holistically, encompassing each and every aspect of this sport, and deals with each as an equally important link in the chain that will ultimately lead to that which is labelled as the *perfect technique*. The majority of studies on kayaking deliver a detailed, often mechanical, description of technique that a particular author recommends, often using professional jargon which is comprehensible, for the most part, only to experts. *The Kayak Coaches' Manifesto* captures the entire body and soul of efficient kayak technique in a language that not only clearly explains to the reader the essence of competitive kayaking technique, but inspires one to go beyond the traditional (and sometimes, boring) comprehension of that which is termed *Olympic Kayaking.*

Michael Fekete,
Sprint Kayak Coach
Strength and Conditioning Specialist
Author of Periodized Strength Training for Sprint Kayaking / Canoeing

Dari Fisher and Imre Kemecsey, together, have perfected a method of teaching the power circles; I am able to appreciate this from both the perspective of an athlete and a strength coach. This style of paddling is not so much about how the end result should look, as much as it is about how it should feel. It concerns itself with learning to access, assess, and work with one's own unique structure, in the attempt to produce speed, power and endurance. This is the ultimate key to success in paddling. I advise anyone interested in this sport to learn, from both Dari and Imre, the secrets of tapping into one's personal and unique potential, and taking paddling to the next level!

Jodi Boates,
Certified Personal Trainer, Certified Core Training Instructor,
Spin Instructor, Weight Training Specialist
Multi Sport Athlete (Surfski and Flatwater Kayaker)
Owner, Jodi Boates Athletics

Correct paddling is often viewed as a complicated puzzle, as so many pieces must fit together in a complex way. It is also confounding on occasion, such as when a paddler who seems not to conform to conventional rules, ultimately excels. Obviously, there exists no one particular set of rules that can be applied to all paddlers in all circumstances, especially when one includes the human psyche. This book, *The Kayak Coaches' Manifesto*, rises above tautologies, just as higher level math rises above the basics of arithmetic and algebra. It deals with the higher level concepts of paddling. Based on the solid groundwork of the principles and practises of Imre Kemecsey, this foundation of ideas sets the scenario for working with the total human athlete, using precepts rather than ritualistic rules; all this in the attempt to create the fastest paddling animal! It is well worth the read.

Earl Metzler

I believe this book is for anyone who propels him/herself forward with a kayak paddle. It is a technical and instructional guide, developed by two very analytical minds, with a strong desire to teach to all levels of kayakers. Though some of the concepts are advanced, they are able to be understood due to the very clear and concise explanations that follow. It is my belief that those of varying levels of ability, from the novice paddler to the elite kayaker, will attain benefit. Dari Fisher has 10 years of experience as a teacher in the public and private secondary school systems; Imre Kemecsey, a former Olympian and National Team coach, holds a Ph.D. among many other qualifications and experiences, which make him a leading world class expert on kayak technique. In fact, Imre's coaching experience spans almost five decades! Imre has coached the entire spectrum from recreational paddlers to world champions, and so his enjoyment of and commitment to coaching is apparent in the broad experience base in which he has involved himself. Furthermore, both Dari and Imre are highly accomplished kayakers themselves, with an intense love of the sport. Their desire to paddle and teach is made apparent throughout *The Kayak Coaches' Manifesto*.

The use of analogies and metaphors throughout the book make these advanced thought-exercises comprehensible to all. As many are aware, if one can imagine oneself achieving a particular motion, this is the first step necessary toward mastery of the movement. The concepts in this book have been designed so that each exercise can be understood, practiced, combined with other exercises, and pieced together to ultimately produce a truly powerful and efficient kayak stroke. I have observed Imre and Dari working together for the last 15 years, during which time they have developed and refined their ideas with respect to the transference of power from the body into the forward motion of the boat. For many (hundreds?! thousands?!) morning and afternoon workouts, Dari would paddle back and forth to the 250 meter marker or 500 meter marker on Burnaby Lake, explaining to Imre the intricacies as to the *feel* of a particular exercise. These two would then commiserate on the matter, refine, and subsequently repeat. I was intrigued by these exercises and joined in on several occasions; within but a few workouts, I was experiencing significant improvements in my own kayak stroke. I may have been viewed as a mere experiment to these two, but the benefits to my paddling have been immeasurable, greatly enhancing my enjoyment of the sport. I firmly believe that the culmination of all of Dari and Imre's workout experiments has lead to the creation of a fine instructional guide on kayak technique.

I have had the pleasure of practicing these exercises on my own on many occasions; the result is undoubtedly that I have experienced tremendous improvements, not only in speed, but also in the efficiency of my stroke. This becomes increasingly clear when one is able to paddle next to another at half the stroke rate, and then pull ahead! I am an easily frustrated individual, and I have had my fair share of less than ideal workouts on the water. Nevertheless, ever since having had the opportunity of learning many of these exercises, now outlined in this manual, I have enjoyed every paddle and workout a great deal more; this is obviously due to the fact that the exercises taught in this manual provide focus, and also assist one in analyzing and comprehending the constructive movements that propel the boat forward. In hindsight, I am still amazed with regards to the dissipation of my own frustration, as it was (and is!) replaced with suitable and constructive focus. These days I often paddle sea kayaks and surfskis. I note, with great enthusiasm, that the techniques discussed in this manifesto are just as applicable and suitable for sea kayakers and surfski paddlers, as they are for flatwater kayakers.

I believe that this is the first book of its kind to be published, in English, at any rate. I have spent many hours in book stores, browsing for a technical guide on kayak stroke technique, and have yet to find one devoted to this topic. All too often, a comprehensive book on kayaking will discuss wing paddles and kayak racing very briefly (and erroneously!) Most books describe the *look* of the various kayaks on the market; however, there is no driver's manual! At last, here is the *learn how to drive* manual of kayaking! I know this guide and the exercises described herein will help any kayaker to reach his/her maximum kayak potential, as it has helped me to reach mine. **Happy paddling!**

David Marchant,
Ph.D. University of British Columbia
James Hogg Research Centre Institute for Heart + Lung Health
St. Paul's Hospital, Vancouver, British Columbia, Canada

A giant thank you, Dari! Your work is brilliant, elegant, eloquent, most precise, and tremendously colourful. Together we can look forward to exploring other innovative and unique exercises and techniques, such as those you have introduced in your book, *The Kayak Coaches' Manifesto*.

Imre Kemecsey
Master Kayak Coach
Ph.D. Sports Psychologist
Olympic Silver Medalist

Dari Y. Fisher is available for lectures, seminars, demonstrations and/or coaching.
Contact information is as follows: Phone: 778-865-3274
Email: kayakcoachesmanifesto@hotmail.com

About the Author

Dari Fisher has been involved in the sport of Flatwater Sprint Kayaking for more than 20 years. He has had many roles over the years including being an athlete, a coach, a personal trainer, and a teacher.

Athletically, some of his highlights consist of winning numerous Provincial Championship, Western Canadian Championship, and National Championship medals. Dari was also a former Canadian Senior National Development Team athlete.

Academically, Dari's post-secondary education commenced at Langara College, in Vancouver, Canada, where he received a Diploma in Coaching & Instruction. Subsequently, he attended the University of British Columbia in Vancouver, where he received a Bachelor of Human Kinetics. Years later he was admitted to the prestigious Urban Diversity Program at York University in Toronto, where he obtained a Bachelor of Education with a specialization in Physical Education.

Vocationally, Dari has developed and worked as a coach at four canoe and kayak clubs throughout Canada; these being the False Creek Racing Canoe Club (Vancouver, BC), the Burnaby Canoe and Kayak Club (Burnaby,BC), the Calgary Canoe Club (Calgary, AB) and the Burloak Canoe Club (Oakville, ON). Career wise, he has completed his eighth year teaching at an inner city high school in Surrey, British Columbia, Canada.